Where Cares Refuse to Stay

ISBN 978-1-935243-11-3

Published in the United States by
Loomis House Press, Northfield, Minnesota

www.loomishousepress.com

Book design by Mark F. Heiman

Where Cares Refuse to Stay

The Story of Pennsylvania's
White Sulphur Spring Hotel

Cliff Saxton, Jr.

LOOMIS HOUSE PRESS

Contents

FOREWORD

Practice hospitality ungrudgingly to one another. As each has received a gift, employ it for one another, as good stewards of God's varied grace... 1 Peter 4: 9-10

More than 30 years ago, Officers' Christian Fellowship (OCF) began looking for a site for an East Coast counterpart to its Colorado conference center, a logical next step in the development of the OCF ministry in serving active-duty military personnel. The search was long and ranged through several eastern states. By the fall of 1977, the Lord's hand had guided OCF to the desired location, and a special relationship began between OCF and the historic former White Sulphur Springs Hotel that continues to unfold today.

When OCF first learned that Paul and Patricia Cochran were seeking a buyer for the 1880s resort they had owned since the mid-1940s, the physical characteristics of the property were apparent—a classic, three-story country inn, a picturesque barn, and other nineteenth-century buildings situated on 630 acres of lush forests in the foothills of the Allegheny Mountains in Bedford County, Pennsylvania. The location also was ideal for OCF in making the ministry accessible to the tens of thousands of military men and women stationed in and around the Washington, D.C. area, just three hours away. Less obvious, however, was a carefully woven mantle of stewardship, generations old, which OCF would take on, a blessing which has contributed much to the ministry's effectiveness.

Over time, White Sulphur Springs basically has had only three stewards: the Colvin family, who managed the hotel starting in 1888 and owned it from 1894 until 1946; the Cochrans; and now OCF. As this book recounts, in every period of stewardship White Sulphur Springs has functioned as a retreat which has drawn guests back time and again, allowing them to get away from the daily grind and refocus on family, friends, and spiritual renewal. OCF inherited this tradition of hospitality, dating back 200 years to those who first discovered the now-fabled spring waters in quiet Milligan's Cove.

The inn could never have been considered luxurious. Compared to major resorts of the time, White Sulphur Springs, while offering excellent food and typical recreational activities, was quite modest in its formative years. Yet once past the rough, unpaved roads they traveled to get there, guests found a very special atmosphere that enabled them, surrounded by the beautiful natural environment and in the company of friendly, caring people, to summon thoughts and feelings which they could not recognize or take time to consider at home. Then, as now, one would be hard-pressed to find a better place for prayer and reflection.

The Lord led OCF to White Sulphur Springs at a time of crisis for the Cochrans prompted by Paul's declining health, in much the same way that the Cochrans were led to rescue the old resort after its owner of many years, Michael Colvin, passed away in 1942. White Sulphur Springs was never a financial bonanza for its owners, and over the years both the Colvins and the Cochrans had opportunities to sell the property to others who would have dramatically changed its character. Instead, they were moved to make personal sacrifices and remain devoted stewards who held on, waiting for a successor who appreciated the total environment that is White Sulphur Springs. What they helped sustain, in effect, was a ministry of service. They provided employment for their own family members and for residents of the surrounding area, and they helped create indelible memories for thousands of guests of all ages. All the while, they preserved a unique slice of America from a quieter time, a facility which is still being of service and now to even farther-reaching effect than in years past.

When OCF assumed ownership, it focused White Sulphur Springs' long tradition of hospitality directly toward military families. These families desperately need a respite from the high-pressure and often-dangerous demands of military life, a respite found in the peace of this special "Place of the Heart" where they are able to listen to the Lord as He heals mothers, fathers, and children, together again in Him. This place also carries forward the military tradition of George Washington that is woven into the history of Bedford County. We are proud to be a respected member of the Bedford community, with the OCF philosophy of compassion and service fitting in well with the natural hospitality of those who have called this beautiful corner of God's creation home for generations.

White Sulphur Springs has become a center for developing Christian leaders for our nation, with an emphasis on cadets and midshipmen from our service academies and civilian universities around the country. OCF is growing, and the new Heritage House main lodge, with its unpretentious design that blends with that of the original buildings, will provide badly needed additional space and updated conference center resources to further our leadership development mission. But the past will always be held dear. There is no question that much of the ministry's growth and success in Milligan's Cove is due to the traditions and stewardship associated with White Sulphur Springs, embodied in the older facilities which have served so well since the 1880s and which will be carefully maintained for continued service in the decades to come.

At Officers' Christian Fellowship, we are keenly aware of those whose faith and hard work helped shape this historic inn. As we strive to build upon the wonderful legacy they have provided, we salute them through this compelling story which speaks to White Sulphur Springs' ongoing role in so many lives as "A Place Apart...A Place of the Heart."

Bruce L. Fister
Lieutenant General, USAF, Retired
Executive Director
Officers' Christian Fellowship

PREFACE

Rural hotels and inns, early predecessors of today's "bed and breakfast" guest houses, were once fixtures of the American landscape, beginning with the first settlers and continuing into the twentieth century. In those times of rugged, primitive roads which often were little more than muddy ruts, the intrepid traveler might spend days covering a distance regarded by today's impatient motorist as a mere commute, and however humble, the roadside hostelry was a welcome sight at the end of a long day's arduous journey.

The inn was often a lodging footnote. More often recalled, in accounts of long-ago travel, are the large hotels which flourished in the bustling cities of the young nation. And yet out in the countryside, isolated from population centers, smaller inns and taverns rose up along the roads, trails, and byways that made up the main commerce routes supporting a growing economy. These establishments could be found at the junctions of prairie roads, along the stage routes of Colonial America and the Old West, or in remote hamlets where the natural wonders and solitude provided a soothing antidote to the pressures and hardships of everyday life. Most were built by local entrepreneurs, often the same pioneers who had first settled the area, and as a result, each had its own unique character.

Many inns and taverns offered only the simplest meals, a generous supply of (generally warm) ale, a crude place to sleep, and care for horses. The cramped lodging quarters were often shared communally, not only with strangers but also with assorted rodents likewise seeking a food supply and refuge from the weather. These early public houses catered mainly to transient overnight guests, many of them teamsters and merchants. At the same time, a number of small inns and hotels sought from the first to provide a higher level of service in the form of better food and more comfortable lodging, allowing travelers to truly relax and prepare themselves for the next leg of their trip. Still others attracted families for longer stays, perhaps for an entire season, and provided the fine dining, lodging, and recreational facilities that came to be expected of first-class resorts. While most inns and taverns functioned throughout the year, inns that had become destinations in their own right often operated on a seasonal schedule, opening in late spring and closing in early fall.

With the United States and its people collectively beginning to recover from the devastating social, emotional, and physical wounds of the Civil War, country inns proliferated in response to the nation's increasing mobility, as well as people's desire to seek healing and spiritual restoration among the wonders of nature. As part of this movement, by the late 1880s, what was then known as the Reed & Lyon White Sulphur Spring in southwestern Pennsylvania's Bedford County had become the centerpiece of a newly opened hotel which would bring a measure of commerce to this quiet farming area, while leaving untouched its slow-paced, bucolic character. Although it was located in convenient proximity to major cities — 80 miles east of Pittsburgh, 100 miles west of Harrisburg, and 140 miles northeast of Washington, D.C. — it was to remain a largely regional inn, remote from the outside world in its secluded mountain cove.

At the time of its construction, the White Sulphur Springs Hotel was typical of dozens of inns built to capitalize on the growing popularity of springs and spas. Mineral baths were a major draw of these resorts, and the waters were praised by many as having curative properties. Situated along a hilly "Packers' Path" which had been frequented by early trappers and traders, White Sulphur

Springs first flourished as the Victorian era was drawing to a close. This was a time in America when stylishly dressed men and women, together with their children and sometimes a small retinue of servants, would disembark at the tiny Sulphur Springs station on the Pennsylvania Railroad, to be conveyed by horse-drawn carriage one and eight-tenths picturesque miles through deep woods to an unassuming two-story (later three-story) hotel. Here they would find a world very different from the urban clamor they left behind, a world that promised guests a "health restorer unequaled" and a retreat "very quiet and restful, with all the comforts and conveniences of more fashionable resorts."

For nearly half a century, the hotel was recognized, both regionally and beyond, for its uniquely aromatic mineral spring water, towering pine trees, and exceptional cuisine, with a gracious hospitality rivaling its competitors. These included the much larger Greenbrier resort which, because of its location in White Sulphur Springs, West Virginia, has often been confused with its more modest Pennsylvania counterpart, once described by owner Paul Cochran as a "country store" by comparison. Guests at Pennsylvania's White Sulphur Springs Hotel could relax in comfortable bentwood hickory rocking chairs scattered about the broad veranda, enjoy a range of outdoor recreation, seek "the great benefit accruing from the sulphur baths, hot or cold" for their various ailments, or simply spend a leisurely day exploring the resort's many acres of unspoiled, sun-dappled forest teeming with wildlife. Hearty meals provided fuel, and an eagerly anticipated reward, for each day's adventures. Satisfied travelers returned again and again, greeting their genial hosts as cordially as members of their own family.

Over time, however, the spa resort era began to fade. The smaller regional inns that once were common in the eastern United States gradually disappeared or were con-verted to other uses as the pace of travel and life in general became more hurried. In the early 1940s, White Sulphur Springs almost passed quietly into history with the death of its longtime owner, Michael Colvin.

And yet the landmark survived, thanks to the devoted stewardship of its three owners, starting in the 1880s with the Colvin family of seven brothers and sisters from Schellsburg, Pennsylvania, of whom Michael was the last survivor. In 1946, with Michael's widow Lorena unable to continue its operation, the property was saved from the lumberman's axe by Paul Cochran, a middle-aged Chicago engineer-industrialist, and his wife Patricia, herself a frequent guest at the hotel since childhood. The Cochrans reopened White Sulphur Springs in 1950 and operated it as a country inn for the next 28 years. By the late 1970s, however, declining health forced them to give up the overwhelming demands of running a resort hotel. An international organization, Officers' Christian Fellowship (OCF), stepped in to begin a new chapter in the history of White Sulphur Springs, transforming it from a tourist hotel into a conference and retreat center dedicated to providing Christian ministry to members of the U.S. military.

Today, while no longer open to the public, the White Sulphur Springs Hotel stands as a compelling reminder of the men and women who have been drawn to this beautiful oasis, and who have had the foresight and commitment to preserve and enhance it for succeeding generations. White Sulphur Springs is still accessed as it was long ago — via wandering two-lane roads offering pleasantly distracting vistas of sweeping valleys, rolling farmland, densely forested hillsides, and rushing mountain streams. The property encompasses more than 1,000 acres heavily wooded with pine, hemlock, oak, maple, and hickory, and may well be the best-preserved example of a traditional small country inn anywhere in the nation. Remarkably, the 1880s hotel with its simple, clapboard facade is little-changed from a century ago, with its curved walnut stair railing, elegant parlors, cozy dining room, and, of course, the same comfortable porch with its nap-inducing rockers. All of the century-old outbuildings also are still used on a daily basis, including a colorful, quirky two-lane bowling alley featuring hand-spotted pins and gravity ball return.

As Officers' Christian Fellowship prepares for the construction of a larger main lodge to accommodate its growing ministry, the future of the classic original hotel building, now known as Harrison House, and the rest of the nineteenth-century White Sulphur Springs facilities remains secure: All will be carefully maintained as the historic treasures they are, continuing to serve as the sentimental focal point of the organization's ministry.

Through the years, the tranquil environment of the hotel has inspired guests and travel writers to record deeply personal impressions of their experiences. Norman Simpson, editor of *Country Inns and Back Roads*, knew he had discovered a special place when he added White Sulphur Springs to his guidebook of historic inns still operating in the early 1970s. He wrote, "We found veneration for good things well done, a preservation of attitudes and responsibilities that seemed to be sloughed off by modern standards, and above all, a wonderful warmth." Libbie Powell, writing in the July 14, 1961 edition of the *Hagerstown* [Maryland] *Daily Mail*, said, "[A] feeling of eternity somehow best describes this place, which is not for those who crave activity and the whirlpool of frustrating events. This is for those who enjoy the antidote of solitude, when one can think and be at peace with one's self. So we shall return when the leaves begin to fall, for the glory of nature abounds, and we found rest for the spirit there."

Now, we invite you to sit back and visit the White Sulphur Springs of an earlier time — to rejoice in the fact that it remains today the same refuge of peace and comfort that it was a century ago, and to gain a sense of its special brand of timeless spiritual and physical rejuvenation, distinguishing it, in the words of a 1950s advertisement, as "The Place Where Cares Refuse To Stay."

BEDFORD AND MANN'S CHOICE AT HISTORY'S CROSSROADS

Hospitality such as that served up in generous portions by White Sulphur Springs is a longtime hallmark of Bedford County, Pennsylvania, where the hotel is located in Milligan's Cove, a short distance from the borough of Mann's Choice, in Harrison Township. From the taverns which sprang up in the 1700s to serve British army soldiers, through the era of the "grand resort" and the birth of the Interstate Highway System, to today's fast-food outlets and chain motels, the region has always extended a genuine welcome to those passing through.

Noted for its abundance of wild game, the area was regularly visited in the early eighteenth century by traders who followed the old Indian trails. The town of Bedford was settled and first came to prominence in the mid-1700s with the construction of Fort Bedford by the British army on the south bank of the Juniata River. Located approximately 100 miles west of Harrisburg, the land originally was laid out as "Raystown" in honor of trader Robert McRae (or "Ray"). In 1759, the British renamed this important military outpost Fort Bedford to honor the politically powerful Duke of Bedford in England. British forces used the fort as a

staging point during the French and Indian War for sorties designed to end French dominance in western Pennsylvania, and it also served as a place for settlers seeking refuge from Indian attacks. In 1769, Fort Bedford became the first British outpost liberated by what were called "American rebels," in this instance James Smith and his "Black Boys," who blacked their faces for battle.

George Washington marched his army of 13,000 militiamen to Bedford in 1794 to subdue the so-called Whiskey Rebellion, an uprising by local citizens angered by a tax on distilled spirits. His commitment to ensuring that the laws of America were obeyed has been viewed by some historians as a cornerstone in establishing the sovereignty

Kinton's Knob, Mann's Choice, Pa.

Rural scene near Milligan's Cove.

of the fledgling federal government formed under the newly ratified Constitution. It also represented one of only two instances when a sitting U.S. President has led an army in the field.

Incorporated in 1795, Bedford was for many years famous for its medicinal springs. At one time, Pennsylvania claimed approximately 50 such springs, some 30 of which were associated with resorts. The Bedford Springs Hotel, the oldest and best-known of the area's spa resorts, hosted its first guests in 1806 and, more than 200 years later, is once again functioning as a public hotel after a period of inac-

Approaching White Suphur Springs.

tivity and subsequent extensive renovations. Other hotels and inns in the area have come and gone, including the spacious Arandale Hotel, razed in the 1970s; the Chalybeate Springs Hotel, whose guests included Rutherford B. Hayes and Benjamin Harrison, and which is still standing although no longer a public inn; and the Fort Bedford Inn, which has been converted to apartments.

Early visitors to Bedford and its resorts often traveled the route which, in 1913, became part of the Lincoln Highway. This 3,389-mile highway, designated U.S. 30 in western Pennsylvania, was the first continuous major east-west route for motor vehicles, connecting New York City's Times Square and San Francisco's Lincoln Park. In October 1940, the opening of the first segment of the Pennsylvania Turnpike, between Irwin and Carlisle, ushered in a new era in motor travel, and hotels and resorts in the Bedford area constructed large billboards on hills overlooking "America's first superhighway" to attract guests. In 1950,

Bedford reported a doubling of its retail sales and commercial growth in the decade since the Turnpike's debut, with local lodging facilities accommodating an average of more than 1,000 travelers and convention guests each night.

Railroads also played a prominent role in the area's growth. Approximately 10 miles southwest of Bedford, across Wills Mountain (named for a Shawnee Indian chief), the town of Mann's Choice was laid out in the late 1860s at what became, in 1871, the temporary southern terminus of the Bedford & Bridgeport Railroad. The route was soon extended further south toward Cumberland, Maryland, and the Baltimore & Ohio Railroad main line, and it became the Bedford Division of the Pennsylvania Railroad system. By 1872, passenger trains were traveling between Cumberland, Bedford, and the PRR's main line at Huntingdon, Pennsylvania, using the tracks of the coal-hauling Huntingdon & Broad Top Mountain Railroad northeast of Bedford. At either end of the line, the major railroads offered connections to cities and towns throughout the country.

Two miles south of Mann's Choice, a modest wooden shelter was erected as the Sulphur Springs railroad station, with trains making the 27-mile Cumberland-Sulphur Springs trip in just under two hours. In 1910, the Pennsylvania Railroad inaugurated twice-daily through passenger service via Bedford to Cumberland along a new, direct route from Altoona, a major hub of railroad operations for the PRR's main east-west line. Well into the 1930s, many White Sulphur Springs Hotel guests availed themselves of this convenient means of transportation, finding it preferable to negotiating the washout-prone local roads.

Although there remains some dispute about the origin of the Mann's Choice name, it is believed that in 1848, Bedford Congressman Job Mann sought to have a post office established in an as-yet unnamed village in Harrison Township. The Post Office Department approved the request and gave the task of naming the area to the Congressman, but before he had a chance to indicate his preference, postal maps were circulated with the interim designation "Mann's Choice," which became permanent.

Regardless of how the town received its unusual name, Mann's Choice grew steadily, its economy bolstered by a business that had been embraced by nearly every township in Bedford County — the tanning of animal skins. By 1880, as area historian Roy F. Kegg noted in *Tales From The Buffalo*, the Mann's Choice tannery had been expanded to an annual capacity of 10,000 sides of finished leather and was the second-largest in the county. The extensive plant, powered by large stationary steam engines attached

Street Scene, Mann's Choice, Pa.

to pulleys, wheels, shafts, and reduction gears which operated machinery throughout the complex, was fueled by coal arriving by railroad from mines to the north. In 1884, as plans for the new White Sulphur Springs Hotel began to take shape, Mann's Choice industries also included a flouring mill, four general stores, a clothing store, a shoemaker, a saddler, two tailors, two blacksmith shops, and two wagon shops, according to Kegg's *A Glimpse of the Foot* ("foot" refers to the area's location at the base of one of the foothills of the Allegheny Mountains). By the turn of the century, the Elk Tanning Co. in Mann's Choice was producing more than 65,000 sides each year, and its oak tanned leather was winning awards at world's fairs in Chicago, New Orleans, St. Louis, and other major cities. The industry flourished until the mid-1920s.

South of Mann's Choice is Milligan's (sometimes spelled "Milliken's") Cove, a secluded, canoe-shaped valley less than 10 miles long and at most a mile wide. Nestled between Wills Mountain and Buffalo Mountain, it bears the name of John Milligan, who was appointed by King George III in 1771 to be a "Justice of the court of general quarter sessions of the peace and of the county court of common pleas for the county of Bedford." Milligan was thought to have first come to the cove on foot via the Packer's Path leading from Bedford across Wills Mountain.

The sulphur springs in the cove were said to have long been a gathering place for American Indians — hallowed ground where inter-tribal disputes were temporarily set aside. Shawnee lore referred to the springs' "healing waters," and arrowheads and other remnants of their presence suggest the Shawnees both knew of and believed in the restorative powers of the springs.

White Sulphur Springs is also located near the historic Forbes Road carved from the wilderness by the British-American troops of General John Forbes during his successful 1758 expedition to occupy French-held Fort Duquesne in western Pennsylvania. It is thought that the springs in Milligan's Cove may have helped sustain Forbes' troops on their difficult journey. According to one legend, the springs were so popular that the army surgeons had to post a guard over the water during their encampment.

Half a century later, Milligan's Cove figured in the local tale of a notorious robber, counterfeiter, and gang leader, Davey Lewis, whose frequent brushes with the law and jail escapes between 1815 and 1820 were portrayed as the acts of a Robin Hood, a man who could not resist temptation and whom "no jail could ever hold." In his book *Davey Lewis*, retired *Bedford Gazette* publisher Ned Frear, a frequent guest at the White Sulphur Springs Hotel since childhood, recounted the exploits of this dashing con man, including an 1819 breakout from the Bedford jail that sent Lewis and two other prisoners "…at a fast pace for Wills Mountain." The chase continued into the woods of Milligan's Cove, and "After a race of between two and three miles, over the roughest ground imaginable," the desperado's companions were finally captured; Lewis himself later surrendered to two armed citizens. "His escape route," Frear wrote, "had taken them over 2,460-foot Kinton's Knob, via the ancient Packer's Path … [The Path] gave the wary traveler a magnificent lookout, commanding little Bedford and the entire surround, and led down into the protected cove where they had been spotted."

Today, Bedford County is a busy center of agriculture and industry, with a wide range of manufacturing enterprises producing everything from bicycles to transformer insulation. Its daily newspaper, the *Bedford Gazette*, is one of the nation's oldest, having been continuously published since 1805. As a Pennsylvania Turnpike exit, Bedford still welcomes travelers to a variety of hotels, motels, and restaurants, as well as points of interest that include a rebuilt

Fort Bedford and a recreated pioneer settlement, Old Bedford Village. In Mann's Choice, the tannery and the railroad that served it are gone, but the core of the town remains active, surrounded by rolling fields of corn, wheat, and other crops. Its Coral Caverns attraction is believed to be the only known fossilized coral reef cavern in the world.

Down the road in Milligan's Cove, while a handful of new houses have been built and farms are fewer, the pace remains leisurely and decidedly friendly. Milk tankers still break the early-morning

VIEW ON ROAD TO STATION. SULPHUR SPRINGS, PA.

THE BRIDGE.
COLVINS WHITE SULPHUR SPRINGS, PA.
NO. 3

quiet as they roam the hilly, winding roads; wildlife and lush vegetation flourish; the white sulphur-infused water of the original Reed & Lyon spring maintains its steady, even flow at a constant 40 degrees; and amidst this tranquil scene, the historic White Sulphur Springs Hotel keeps its timeless vigil.

EARLY MILLIGAN'S COVE BOARDING HOUSES AND THE MAY FAMILY

The sequence of events which led to the construction of a spa resort in Milligan's Cove began with the gradual transformation of the area in the 1800s from a brief stop along the Packers' Path into a small settlement of seasonally operated boarding houses.

Lost to time is the exact date on which the very first inn opened for business in the cove. According to descendants of families who settled in the area long ago, at some point in the eighteenth century — some accounts suggest a date in the 1770s, others say much earlier — a two-story log wayside tavern was constructed in a hillside clearing a quarter-mile above the site of the current hotel, on land warranted to Peter Wertz. It is said that it, too, may have been called the White Sulphur Springs Hotel. Originally a way station for drovers using the Packers' Path along the crest of Wills Mountain, the building was refurbished in later years to provide 16 rooms for guests coming to "take the waters" at the area's springs. The structure apparently remained in use through much of the 1800s, and its ruins were still visible well into the middle of the twentieth century, when Paul and Patricia Cochran became the owners of White Sulphur Springs. A few of the original

The original White Sulphur Springs two-story log inn and tavern, still standing c. 1900.

Kinton's Knob — postcard showing the route of the Packer's Path used by drovers passing through Milligan's Cove.

The remains of the first May home in Milligan's Cove, thought to have served as Daniel May, Jr.'s original log boarding house; 1911.

hand-hewn timbers, saved in a sheep barn built by the Cochrans, can be seen today supporting the ceiling of the White Sulphur Springs museum in the small cottage next to the main hotel building. Other timbers are believed to be part of the hotel's picturesque horse barn. Little else is known about this early log structure, which started the tradition of hospitality in the cove that continues today.

By the 1870s, in recognition of the growing popularity of the area's several mineral springs, a number of farms in Milligan's Cove had been turned into what became well-regarded boarding houses or small hotels as their owners sought to supplement their income by accepting paying guests. Most, and perhaps all, were owned by the May family, whose members had been among the first settlers of the area. Daniel May, the family patriarch, had arrived

in the cove in the late 1700s, and his descendants established at least three popular destinations for early travelers.

Daniel May, Jr. operated a boarding house in a log structure which, toward the end of its existence in the late 1880s, had fallen into serious disrepair. Daniel's third wife was the former Charlotte Reed, whose birth family would become involved in the construction of today's White Sulphur Springs Hotel building. Following Daniel's death in the late 1870s, Charlotte continued to operate the boarding house, and the 1880 census indicates that three boarders were residing there.

Two of Daniel May, Jr.'s sons also operated boarding houses on their nearby farms.

Closest to the site of today's White Sulphur Springs was the 1874 home of Daniel's son Hezekiah E. May. *The History of Bedford, Somerset, and Fulton Counties*, published in 1884, noted that "H.E. May has always resided near his old home, and, by prudent economy and well-directed industry, has gained wealth and prosperity. The celebrated White Sulphur spring is but a short distance from his house, and Mr. May's large and commodious residence is

ARLINGTON COTTAGE HOTEL,
H. E. MAY, Proprietor,
WHITE SULPHUR SPRINGS, PA.
10 MILES SOUTH OF BEDFORD.

This Cottage Hotel has recently been refurnished and is fitted for the accommodation of a large number of health-seeking visitors. It has large airy rooms and porchs, and fine shade trees. Sulphur and Iron Water, clear and abundant, the richest in minerals in the valley and in nice shady places with rustic seats. Good places for game and fishing.

Buss runs to meet trains for all visitors.

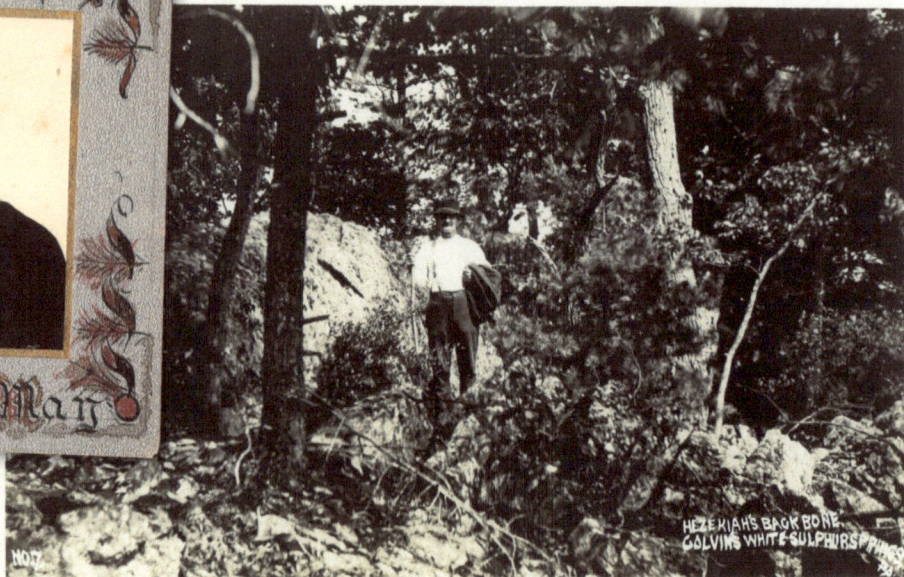

Drawn portrait of Abraham and Sarah May;
Hezekiah's Backbone — postcard showing a local
geologic feature and Hezekiah May himself.

a favorite resort with summer tourists. His home is visited by people from all parts of the country, and no one who has once enjoyed its hospitality fails to wish to come again." Known as the Arlington Cottage Hotel, it charged rates of "$1.00 Per Day, or $5.25 Per Week, with half price for children under 12 years of age." Hezekiah May's home still stands and is now used by Officers' Christian Fellowship for staff housing.

After his honorable discharge from Civil War military service, Hezekiah's brother Abraham erected a house in Milligan's Cove in 1872 "for the accommodation of summer boarders, and every summer it is filled with seekers after health and pleasure. The surrounding scenery is beautiful, and every feature of the valley attractive." Abraham M. May's boarding house was located slightly uphill from Hezekiah's home, and it was known as the Mountain House and sometimes the "upper house." It featured two smaller springs, one a white sulphur spring used for bathing and the other "black sulphur," containing more iron. John Egolf, great-great grandson of Abraham May, explored the abandoned Mountain House as a child. He recalled the pine-sided building as having two large rooms on the first level, with a pot-bellied stove, and four bedrooms upstairs.

By the 1880s, the era of the small, family-run combination farm and boarding house in Milligan's Cove was winding down. Given the growing popularity of the area as a tourist destination, it is not surprising that plans were evolving for a larger inn that would eventually replace the various separate small facilities.

AT WHITE SULPHUR.

A Visitor Who Is Enchanted With its Beauty and its Healthfulness.

GAZETTE Correspondence.

SULPHUR SPRINGS, July 20 — On arriving at this point the first evening we could exclaim in thunder tones as follows:

> Shut the door gently,
> Bridle the breath,
> I've got the sick-headache
> Nigh unto death.

But after a pleasant sojourn at the "Mountain House" with our amiable host and hostess Mr. and Mrs. A. M. May, and after partaking freely of the sparkling mineral waters which burst forth almost at their very door, we feel almost as if we had been born anew, or at least that life still had its charms.

Nowhere in all this broad land can you find such accommodations, healthful climate, good mineral water and fine, romantic scenery—for so moderate an outlay of money. Mr. May and lady seem to vie with each other as to which can be the more pleasant and painstaking in seeing that their guests are nicely cared for, and so endeared to their guests have they become that one not un-frequently hears Mrs. May addressed as "mother" by some of the visitors. A friend remarked to-day that he never saw such an agreeable crowd at one boarding house in his life, and we are of the same opinion. None of your dividing off in separate society circles here, but from early in the morn until the setting of the sun they can be seen either at the spring, in the dancing hall or promenading through the leafy groves, almost an undivided crowd.

We have stopping at this house the charming maidens just making their debut into society and ready without a moment's warning to plunge Cupid's dart into the susceptible young man, who though often (perhaps) has felt its pangs, is still willing to be a target. Then we have young men fresh from college life, trying to recuperate their constitutions somewhat broken up by over-study. Another somewhat striking feature about these Springs, or at least the Mountain House, is that the festive mosquito never puts in an appearance so that you don't have to sleep under a "mosquito bar" and have your breath strained in order to exist until morning.

On first coming here, the atmosphere seemed to have a drowsy effect, and you feel as if you could lie down and sleep until resurrection morn, but after a sojourn of a few days you feel as refreshed and as cheerful as anyone could desire to be.

As I write the strains of music from the dancing hall and peals of merry laughter breaking in upon the stillness of night warn me that if I would participate in the giddy whirl I had better get up and whirl. CHARLIE

July 30, 1886, *Bedford Gazette*

The Reed & Lyon White Sulphur Spring before the construction of the hotel, 1882.

The Beginnings of the White Sulphur Springs Hotel

The story of the construction and the first 60 years of the White Sulphur Springs Hotel primarily involves two families — the Reeds and the Colvins.

The February 1814 marriage of Michael Reed and Elizabeth Schell of Schellsburg, near Bedford, produced 10 children, including John P., Jacob, Margaretta (or Margaret), and Charlotta (or Charlotte), all four of whom would figure in the earliest years of White Sulphur Springs. Michael learned cabinet-making early in life with his father at their home in Franklin County, Pennsylvania. When of age, he drifted some 70 miles west to settle in the small village of Schellsburg, soon marrying into the town's founding Schell family. According to an account in the *History and Genealogy of the Reed Family* published in 1929, Michael's early schooling was limited, so he became a self-made man, studied surveying and eventually worked as both an engineer and a surveyor. He built his own surveying instruments and used them in laying out the Bedford and Hollidaysburg Turnpike. "His business ventures were successful from the beginning, and in time he became the leading and most successful and enterprising business man of the town. He prospered with the town's growth and development, and was one of its wealthiest citizens."

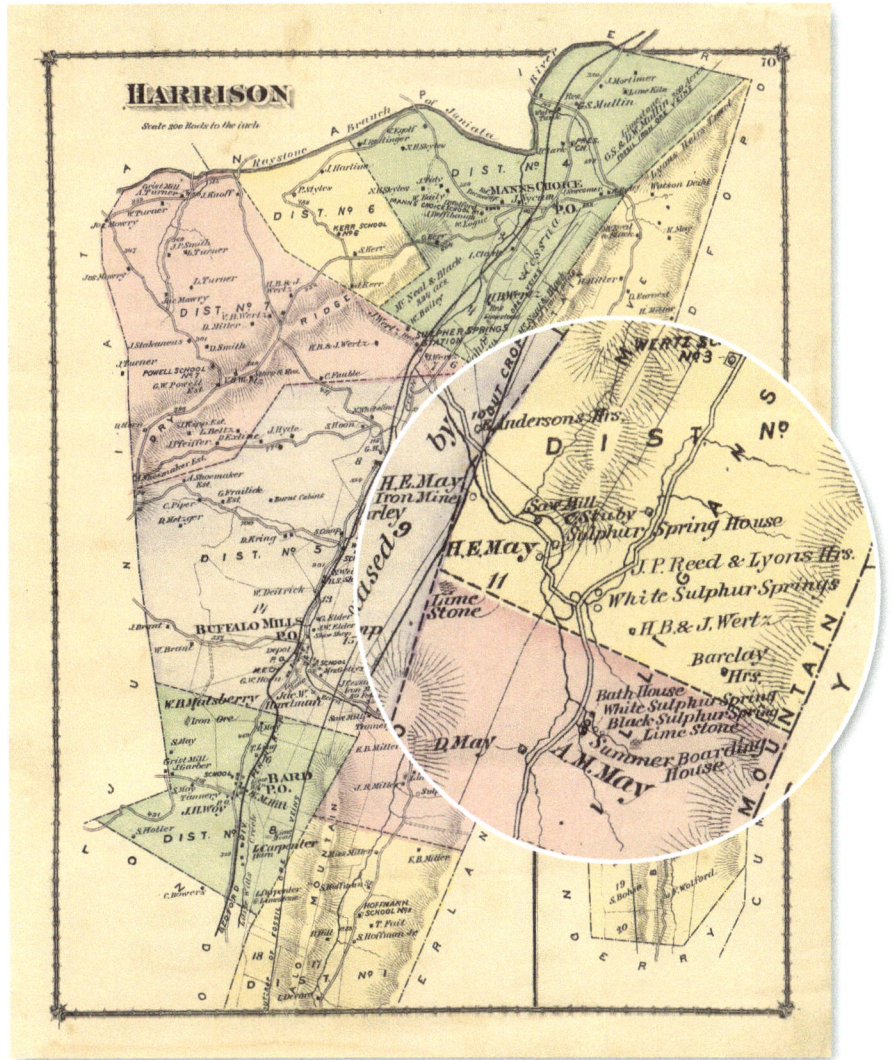

Harrison Township in 1877, showing May and Reed holdings as well as numerous springs.

The Colvin Family at White Sulphur Springs, c. 1894; Back: Nina, Phebe, Michael, Ella, Annie; Front: Reuben, Margaretta (Reed), Ross, Emma.

The Colvins had been respected members of the Schellsburg, Pennsylvania, community for many years, ever since George Colvin, a farmer and hotelkeeper by occupation, moved to the town from Baltimore in 1832 and married Elizabeth McDowell. According to an abstract provided by the Bedford County Historical Society, Colvin was something of a land baron, owning various properties which included "the Western Hotel, one of the most substantial houses in Schellsburg, two nearby farms, and a tavern house and a lot in the borough of Somerset." On June 17, 1847, Margaretta Reed, daughter of Michael and Elizabeth, and Reuben R. Colvin, one of George's sons, were married. Following George's death in 1848, Reuben and Margaretta inherited his 163-acre farm along the road from Bedford to Schellsburg. They had five daughters and five sons; two sons did not survive infancy and a third died at 21.

Ultimately, it was a combination of an investment opportunity, family experience in the innkeeping business, and an abundance of family members in search of employment that led the Reeds and Colvins to their involvement in the White Sulphur Springs story. Although the seeds of the project were planted in 1871, it would take another 16 years before the first guests checked in at the front desk of the new hotel building. It all started, as do many great American stories, with land ownership.

The White Sulphur Springs Hotel building is located on a parcel of "50 acres more or less" known as the Sulphur Springs Hotel Property. The land originally was owned by Daniel May, Jr. and his first wife Rachel who, in 1847, conveyed it to William Lyon and Samuel M. Barclay, both prominent Bedford attorneys. Following Barclay's death, John P. and Jacob Reed, the sons of Michael and Elizabeth, became owners of Barclay's interest in the tract and also acquired one-sixth of Lyon's holding. When Jacob's business failed, John P. Reed, himself a Bedford attorney, acquired his brother's share in 1871, and John P. Reed and Lyon thus became partners in owning what would thereafter be referred to as the Reed & Lyon White Sulphur Spring.

Tax records from those years indicate that the property had no improvements or structures on it, although the spring itself was well-known in the area. Members of the Reed and Lyon families continued to own the property, with John P. Reed and William Lyon's widow, Catharine, apparently pooling their resources in the mid-1880s to erect the White Sulphur Springs Hotel building on the site. Following Catharine Lyon's death in 1889, her son George inherited her share of the property, and on March 3, 1894, John P. Reed and George M. Lyon sold the land

R. Ross Colvin, c. 1888

and buildings for $10,000 to the Colvin family, which had managed the hotel under a rental agreement since 1888. The new ownership was held in shares by six of the seven Colvin siblings who operated the property: one-fourth each by brothers Ross and Michael Colvin, and one-eighth each by sisters Annie, Ella, Nina, and Phebe. The fifth and oldest Colvin sister, Emma, apparently had no financial interest in the hotel, although she lived and worked there alongside her brothers and sisters throughout the remainder of her life.

An adjoining parcel southeast of the Sulphur Springs Hotel Property, known as the "Peter Wertz Sulphur Springs Tract," was the site of the early White Sulphur Springs log hotel. For many years, this parcel remained in the Wertz family, passing first to Peter's sons Hugh and James. In 1894, the entire tract came under the ownership of Sarah Jane Egolf, the daughter of James Wertz, and she in turn sold it in January 1901 to John H. Rudy, a local lumberman, and his wife Sarah. Two months later, on March 30, 1901, the Colvin brothers purchased slightly over 50 acres of the parcel from the Rudys for $1,200, increasing the Colvins' total White Sulphur Springs land holdings to almost 100 acres.

THE CONSTRUCTION OF A NEW HOTEL

It is unclear precisely how and when the decision was reached to construct a relatively large hotel building in rural Milligan's Cove. However, events converged to open the door for such an enterprise.

By the 1880s, the Peter Wertz tavern had closed; Abraham and Hezekiah May were approaching retirement age; their father, Daniel May, Jr. had died in 1878; and widow Charlotte May's log boarding house was deteriorating. In view of the proven popularity of the smaller hotels, the undeveloped White Sulphur Springs property owned by John P. Reed and Mrs. Catharine Lyon, widow of William

Lyon, clearly represented an investment opportunity.

The co-owners of the property probably never saw themselves as innkeepers. Reed in 1883 was 66 years old and had a law practice in Bedford, while Mrs. Lyon by this time was living in Chicago; certainly they knew that they would have to rely on others if the new hotel was to succeed. Although Mrs. Lyon undoubtedly played a financial role in the new venture in hopes of increasing the value of the investment for her descendants, it is likely that Reed, with a slight majority ownership and because he resided in Pennsylvania, took the lead in the project,

The original two-story hotel, c. 1890.

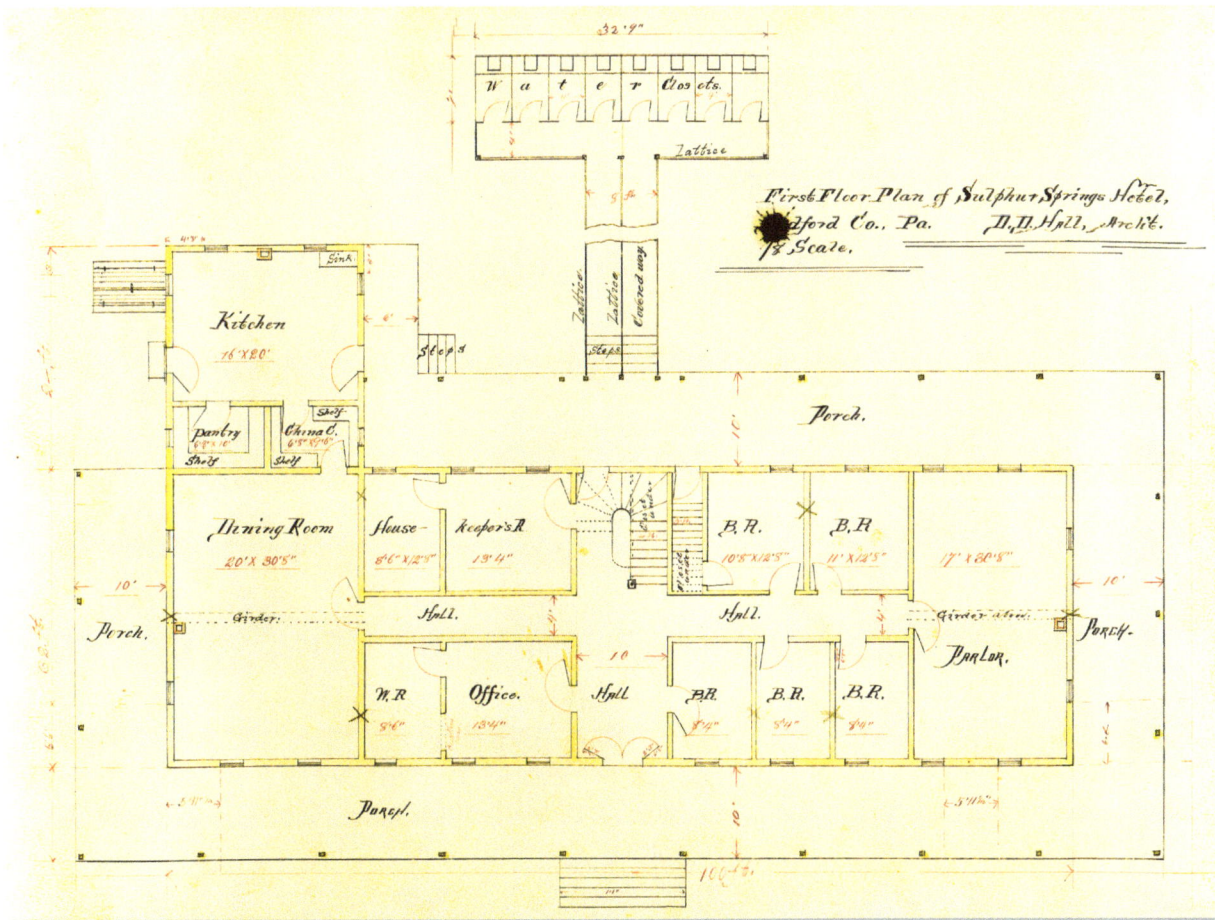

First Floor Plan of Sulphur Springs Hotel, [B]dford Co., Pa. D.D. Hall, Arch't. 1/8 Scale.

both to further his own financial interests and to assist the widow of his longtime friend. For Reed, however, the new hotel was only one of a number of local investments, and while he was often a guest at the new White Sulphur Springs Hotel, his backing of its construction with Mrs. Lyon is not mentioned in the Reed family history or in a lengthy notice published after his death in 1908.

Sometime in the 1880s, probably in 1884-1886, John Reed and Catharine Lyon authorized construction of the hotel and several out-buildings, including a two-story cottage next door which served as an office and had four bedrooms. The main floor of the hotel contained the front desk, dining room and kitchen, five bedrooms, a parlor at the north end, and housekeeping rooms. There were 19 bedrooms on the second floor. Sanitary facilities were outdoor; an eight-stall water closet was situated at the end of an open-sided covered walkway extending behind the hotel at the first-floor level.

Original plans for the first two floors and exterior designs of the new hotel bear the signature of D.D. Hall,

Architect. Local historian Roy Kegg identified the hotel's "Master Builder" as Watson Diehl, Abraham May's son-in-law and a skilled local carpenter who specialized in building barns. Because the plans are not dated, various years have been cited for the facility's opening. Hotel registers and newspaper articles help to pinpoint the summer of 1887 as the first season of official operation by the new resort, although it may have been functioning on a limited basis somewhat earlier. The first guest, Alex Lowry of Butler, Pennsylvania, signed the hotel's register on June 17, 1887. That same day, the *Bedford Gazette* published the following item:

"The summer visitors to the Sulphur Springs, in Milliken's Cove, will be glad to learn that the new hotel, erected by Reed and Lyon, adjoining the spring, is completed and ready to receive guests. The building is 100 feet long and 34 feet wide, two stories in height, with porches 10 feet wide. It has twenty-eight commodious bed-rooms for the entertainment of guests.

The furniture, bedding &c. are all new. Visitors seeking accommodations near the spring will find the new hotel just what has long been needed."

With a grand new building rising in the middle of the pine forests of Milligan's Cove, the owners turned their attention to arranging day-to-day oversight of the White Sulphur Springs Hotel. With John Reed still practicing law and Catharine Lyon nearly 600 miles away in Chicago, they turned to family members for assistance. First to be tapped — and possibly the intended candidate ever since the hotel was first envisioned — was Charlotte May, sister of co-owner John Reed and widow of Daniel May Jr., who was still taking in boarders to make ends meet. On May 26, 1887, three weeks before the new hotel formally opened, Charlotte was contracted by her brother and Catharine Lyon to manage the facility. Under their agreement, she was "… to move into the said house as tenant under the said Reed & Lyon and occupy the same until the first day of

---

SULPHUR SPRING HOTEL.

——

Milliken's Cove, Bedford Co., Pa.

Reed & Lyon have just had erected a large Hotel among the pines and furnished the same from top to bottom with new oak furniture and new beds. The best water in the United States, Sulphur and Iron. Ready for guests June 20, 1887. Terms $7 and up. Address, Mrs. Charlotte May, Mann's Choice, Bedford Co., Pa.

June 17 w3

Front Elevation of Sulphur Springs Hotel, Bedford Co., Pa.   ⅛ Scale. D. H. Hall, Arch't.

April 1888, and run and use and manage the same as a boarding house hotel, using her best discretion and ability to make the same a popular resort for invalids, guests and others seeking a place for rest and restoration of health."

Charlotte was to be compensated one-half of the net profits of the business, but not less than $300 "so as to secure her from loss, in abandoning the house she kept last season," presumably referring to the nearby Daniel May log boarding house she had formerly operated. The owners specified a minimum boarding charge of $7 per week, and the agreement also listed new furnishings being entrusted to their manager. These included 21 pairs of Plymouth Blankets, 34 yards of table linen, "30 Ewers & Basins & 30 Chambers, 18 comforts, and 6 cots," with a value of $338.03. Charlotte's new role was confirmed by a brief Bedford newspaper item in May 1887 that noted "Miss Lottie May, who for many years has conducted one of the most popular houses at the Springs, will have charge of the new hotel."

The spring house and original two-story hotel, c. 1890.

The now three-story
hotel (1901)

Colvin family and staff, Back: ?, Emma, Margaretta, ?, Annie, ?; Front: Ross, Phebe, ?, Michael, ?, ?, Ella, c. 1900

Charlotte May, when she took on the job of running the new hotel, was in her late 50s, considered an advanced age for that time, and while accustomed to taking care of a few boarders in her home, she may have soon found the needs of managing a 28-room hotel overwhelming and let the owners know they needed to find a more permanent oversight arrangement.

A solution was again found within the family. In the late 1880s, among the children of Charlotte's sister Margaretta (Margaret) Reed Colvin and her husband Reuben was a son Ross, nearing 30, who was probably casting about in search of a direction for his life. Their middle son, Jacob Reed Colvin, died in 1888 at the age of 21, while the Colvins' youngest son, Michael, had recently graduated from high school in Schellsburg. The couple's five unmarried daughters all were older than Michael, ranging in age from 24 to 38. In an era where gainful employment opportunities for women in a rural area were scarce, the operation of boarding houses and hotels represented one of the few viable options. As such, all of the Colvin family members had likely grown up with at least some involvement in George Colvin's hotel business in Schellsburg and were likely candidates to become involved in the new Milligan's Cove enterprise.

It is easy to envision the scenario of Reuben Colvin suggesting to son Ross that he contact his Aunt Charlotte to see if she needed help running the new hotel — help which might also provide employment for Reuben's other children. Conversely, Charlotte may have taken the initiative to ask her sister Margaret for the family's assistance in managing the hotel. In view of the one-year length of Charlotte's contract, it is also possible that the Reeds and Colvins had agreed, before construction began, on the family members' various roles and the timing of those roles, with Michael becoming available to work full-time starting with the 1888 summer season after completing school. Whatever the circumstances, after her agreement with John Reed and Catharine Lyon ended in April 1888, Charlotte left White Sulphur Springs, and the Colvins moved in under a rental agreement with the owners.

Over the next decade, the White Sulphur Springs facilities were expanded significantly. In July 1894, the third floor of the hotel, containing 20 guest rooms and apparently built using the second floor as a template, was opened, and second- and third-floor bedrooms were added over an extended kitchen area at the south end of the hotel. At about the same time, a center wing was added containing hot and cold sulphur baths as well as much-welcomed indoor sanitary facilities, enabling the hotel to advertise bathrooms on each floor for the first time. (Installation of individual guest room baths was still half a century away.) The modifications increased hotel lodging capacity to 125 guests, prompting enlargement of the first-floor dining room by two-thirds. It is likely that the various improvements were underwritten by the owners on the advice of Ross and Michael Colvin, based on their experiences with increasing business volume.

The Colvins continued the rental arrangement until March 1894, when they purchased the hotel and surrounding acreage from John Reed and George M. Lyon. At this point, Ross was in his mid-30s and Michael in his mid-20s, and the two initially functioned as co-proprietors of the hotel and partners in the firm of R.R. and M.S. Colvin. Throughout the Colvin family's ownership of White Sulphur Springs, it was always indicated on rate cards and other literature that the hotel's first year was 1888, when their own rental agreement began, and not 1887, when Charlotte May became the first manager. The Colvins made further improvements to the resort, adding the two-lane bowling alley building about 1897.

The Colvin brothers were the only family members

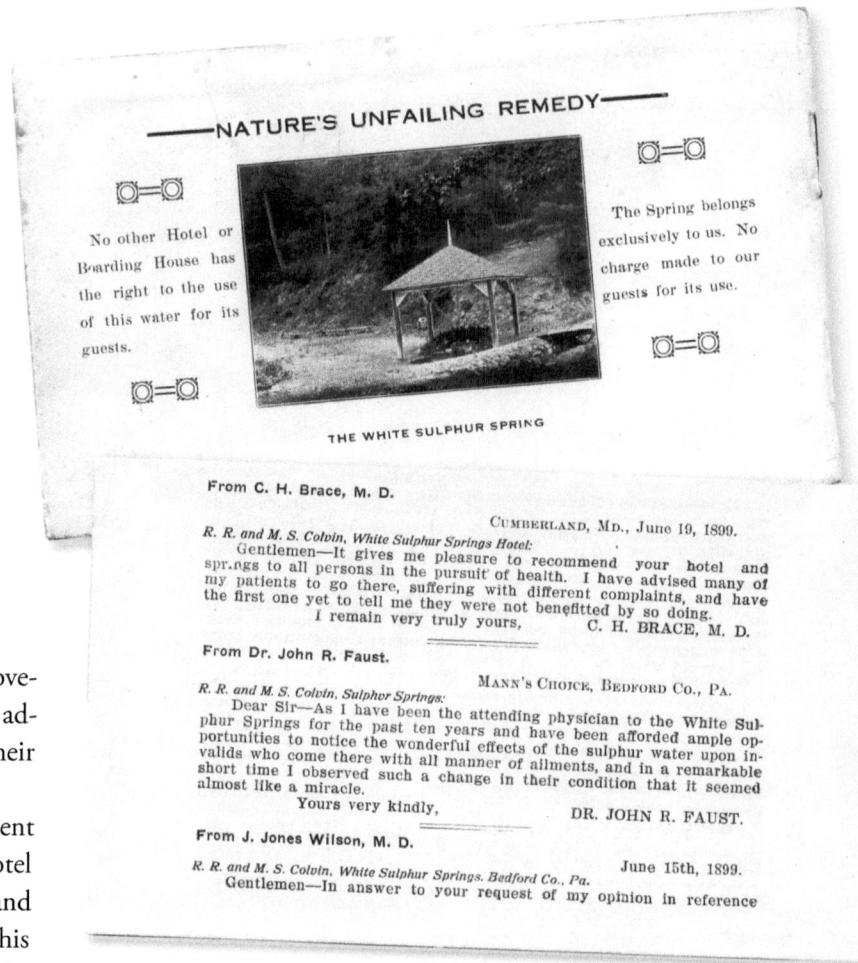

Pages from a Colvin promotional brochure, c. 1900.

ever referenced in White Sulphur Springs brochures and advertisements, operating the facility as "R.R. and M.S. Colvin, Proprietors." Nevertheless, the sisters apparently actively assisted their brothers in various capacities, including food service and housekeeping. Subsequent owner Patricia Cochran's recollections of the sisters dated from her first visit to White Sulphur Springs in 1910; by then, the fourth-born Colvin sister, Nina, had passed away, but

The Colvins in Atlantic City, N.J. c. 1920, Back: Phebe, Ella, Michael's wife Lorena. Front: Emma, Annie, Michael.

the four remaining sisters were all still involved with the hotel. Their personalities were unique.

"Miss Emma was the eldest and the only one not financially interested in the hotel," Mrs. Cochran recalled. "She had sharp features and a sharp tongue to go with them. She never used the sharp tongue on me, but I heard her sitting on the front porch when a certain car would go by, and she would say, 'She's nothing but a snip!' And she would say it in such a way that you'd think she was swearing!"

Emma Colvin figured into another incident which occurred when Patricia was still single and a guest at the hotel with her mother. A beau from New York City, John, came to White Sulphur Springs to see Patricia, for some reason bringing along his mother.

"The long upstairs hallway on the second floor needed a new runner, and one had been ordered," Mrs. Cochran remembered. "But at the top of the stairway there was a great big hole in the carpet. At about 3 o'clock in the afternoon, John and his mother arrived, and I was bringing them upstairs to show them to their room. And as we made the last turn at the top of the stairs, here was Miss Emma, little old Miss Emma, down on her hands and knees trying to darn up this big hole in the carpet, which was a nice first impression for anyone coming from New York."

"Miss Annie was a little chubby person with her hair drawn up tight on her head in a little topknot, and she was the one who took care of the food department in the kitchen." Anna E. Colvin's 1920 obituary reported, "Through all of her years at this popular resort she has had an important and responsible place in conducting the hotel, and its high reputation for superior cuisine and its table service is due in no small degree to her ability and efficiency."

Mrs. Cochran said that "Miss Phebe would go in the rag bag and haul out all these old towels that had great big holes in them — then after the evening meal, she'd take them out on the porch and she'd sit there and darn away these awful holes. The other guests would come to Michael and say, 'Mr. Colvin, how can you make that poor old lady mend those awful rags?' And he'd swear and say, 'Well, stop her if you can!'"

"Miss Ella was a very handsome, beautiful, tall woman, with the most beautiful eyes that looked like pansies. They were set tilted in her face."

Lorena Smelker Colvin on the porch of the cottage, c. 1920.

Change came to the family circle starting in 1911, the year in which both Ross and Michael Colvin married. Michael wed former bank teller Lorena Smelker of Newton Hamilton, Pennsylvania, on October 25, and one month later, on Thanksgiving Day, Ross married Virginia Hurley of Altoona. Virginia, then 29, was 23 years younger than Ross (there is some evidence that the groom may have misrepresented his age to his bride). She was also substantially younger than all of the Colvin sisters, the eldest of whom was then 61, a disparity which might not have been well-received and may explain the absence of all of the groom's siblings from his wedding. It is also possible that the age difference created friction in the close living quarters at White Sulphur Springs. The sisters, while most had ownership shares in the hotel, were never referred to as owners or proprietors, and after 20-plus years of working in largely anonymous and arduous support functions, they

may not have taken kindly to the new, younger wife suddenly occupying a role seemingly superior to theirs.

There is also reason to believe that Virginia's relocation to remote Milligan's Cove from bustling city of Altoona, where she had been employed in an influential and visible department store administrative position, may have proven less than satisfying for her. Following Ross Colvin's death in 1923, his widow became associate editor of the *Bedford Inquirer*, and some years later, a newspaper colleague interviewed Virginia Colvin about the "old days" of the hotel.

"In the days when there was a summer post office at the Springs," the account noted, "she was named assistant to her husband, the late Ross Colvin, and clerked at the store, which sold candy and soft drinks. The little building housed the bowling alley, a favorite evening pastime with guests and young folk from the neighboring communities. It was not uncommon for her to keep score until midnight on a busy evening for the bowlers who usually rolled the big pins. Some high scores were made on the alleys in those days and Mrs. Colvin remembers one time that she tied the Cumberland duck pin champion in a series of ten games."

Despite her occasional bowling triumphs, newlywed Virginia Colvin may well have become disenchanted with manually setting pins and recording scores for hours on

A beautiful retreat among the pines and mountains of Bedford county, Pa.

A large three story hotel, with broad verandas surrounding the same

White Sulphur Springs Hotel,

The sulphur and iron water is unsurpassed.   Terms from $7. to $10. per week,

$1.50 per day.   Open early and late in the season.

R. R. COLVIN.   **M. S. COLVIN.**

BEDFORD CO.

Sulphur Springs, Penna., _____ 189

Thursday dinner

Roast beef, Pot pie, Tomatoes

Potatoes dressed with Milk

____ with wine Sauce, Black

____ries and Watermellon,

____read coffee and butter

Howards Photos   COR. 8 TH AVE. & 12TH ST. ALTOONA, PA.

COLVIN'S HOTEL - SULPHUR SPRINGS, PA.

Colvin letterhead, a Colvin-era cabinet card and a hotel promotional postcard.

The White Sulphur Springs bowling alley, 1930s (exterior) and today (interior).

end in the cramped, dark building. In any event, on June 23, 1913, just 19 months after his marriage, Ross Colvin severed his official ties with White Sulphur Springs. Selling his entire interest in the hotel and two tracts of surrounding land to sisters Annie, Phebe, and Ella Colvin for $7,000, he dissolved the R.R. and M.S. Colvin firm, and relocated with his wife to a farm he had purchased near Brooks Mills, Pennsylvania. In subsequent years, Ross and

Virginia were regular guests at the hotel, often bringing friends with them.

After the Ross Colvins moved out, Michael, his wife Lorena, and the Colvin sisters continued to operate and live at White Sulphur Springs, with Emma apparently retiring from active involvement around 1920. Two sons were born to Michael and Lorena early in their marriage, but neither survived the first years of life.

Enjoying the Hospitality of Colvin's White Sulphur Springs

White Sulphur Springs, also known as Colvin's White Sulphur Springs, retained the informality and cordiality that had attracted guests through the years to the smaller Milligan's Cove boarding houses operated by the Mays. Like its predecessors, White Sulphur Springs for many years was a summer-only inn and resort, and as such, its hot water heating system was not designed for the extremes of Pennsylvania winters. An 1890 advertisement carrying R. Ross Colvin's name noted that the hotel would be open from May 15 to October 1, with "reduced rates prior to June 1 and after September 1," a typical schedule for many years. Still, hotel records indicate that visitors were occasionally accommodated in the off season. Lodging terms were from $7 to $10 a week, or $1.50 per day, and a pamphlet published by the Colvins in the early 1900s warned that "unruly children will not be tolerated."

PENNSYLVANIA RAILROAD.—Branches Continued. 139

BEDFORD DIVISION.
Wm. H. Brown, Superintendent, Bedford, Pa.

STATIONS.	Mls	Accom.	Mail.
Lve. **Huntingdon** [1]			8 00 A.M.
" **Mt. Dallas** [2]	0		11 15 "
" Ashcom.............	2		11 21 "
" Lutzville..............	3		11 26 "
" Jameson	5		11 33 "
" **Bedford**.............	8	7 30 A.M.	11 50 A.M.
" Wolfsburg.............	11	7 42 "	12 02 NO'N
" Napier.............	13	7 50 "	12 10 P. M.
" Mann's Choice.........	16	8 03 "	12 23 "
" Sulphur Springs.........	18	8 11 "	12 31 "
" Buffalo Mills..........	21	8 23 "	12 42 "
" Londonderry........ .	22	8 29 "	12 48 "
" Preston	27	8 48 "	1 06 "
" Wills Creek...........	30	9 00 "	1 18 "
" **Bridgeport** [3].........	31	9 03 "	1 21 "
" Cook's Mill...........	36	...	...
" State Line.............	39	...	...
Arr. **Cumberland** [4]........	45	9 55 A.M.	2 08 P.M.

STATIONS.	Mls	Mail.	Accom.	CONNECTIONS.
Lve. **Cumberland** [4]........	0	9 35 A.M.	5 10 P.M.	
" State Line............	6	...	...	
" Cook's Mill............	9	...	...	
" **Bridgeport** [3]........	14	10 25 "	6 00 "	[1] With Main Line Pennsylvania Railroad.
" Wills Creek............	15	10 28 "	6 03 "	
" Preston	18	10 39 "	6 15 "	[2] With Huntingdon and Broad Top Railroad.
" Londonderry......... ..	23	10 56 "	6 33 "	
" Buffalo Mills..........	24	11 02 "	6 39 "	[3] With Pittsburg, Washington and
" Sulphur Springs........	27	11 13 "	6 50 "	more Railroad.
" Mann's Choice.........	29	11 20 "	6 58 "	
" Napier	32	11 31 "		
" Wolfsburg.............	34	11 39 "		
" **Bedford**	37	11 55 A.		
" Jameson	40	12 02 N(		
" Lutzville.............	42	12 09 P		
" Ashcom..............	44	12 14		
" **Mt. Dallas** [2]........	45	12 25		
Arr. **Huntingdon** [1]........		3 20		

KINTONS KNOB. P.R.R.
SULPHUR SPRINGS, PA.

1872 rail schedule; horse-drawn carriage at the station (1907); the original Sulphur Springs station.

Adams Express Company.

Inward Way-Bill and Delivery Book

Form 97 B.

Hay ride, c. 1895; Adams Express Delivery Book, c. 1900 — Adams brought trunks and packages to the hotel; tennis players and other guests, c. 1890.

Ross Colvin (standing), his wife Virginia (standing, hatless) and a crew of smiling guests at the newly constructed Sulphur Springs depot, c. 1912.

Guests were initially met at the Sulphur Springs railroad station by a coach and four, and by the late 1800s, railroads were operating excursion packages that involved the Colvin hotel. According to an 1899 railroad guide, at Sulphur Springs, "… the fine local reputation heretofore enjoyed by this health-creating resort has now become universal. The location is exceedingly picturesque and romantic. The water contains a combination of iron, sulphur, and other mineral ingredients of medicinal value." Excursion fares ranged from 50 cents (from Bedford) to $7.05 (from "Pittsburg"). In 1912, apparently with the expectation of increased passenger and freight volume, the Pennsylvania Railroad replaced the simple wooden Sulphur Springs shelter with a small but attractive enclosed and roofed depot building. Hotel registers occasionally noted "auto" beside a guest's name, although the train was the preferred method of travel during the resort's first

three decades. A former waitress at White Sulphur Springs who lived near the railroad tracks, Virginia Leydig Lankey, remembered how exciting it was as a very young child to glimpse, through the windows of the slow-moving train, the stylish dresses and hats worn by ladies bound for the resort. On still days, hotel guests rocking on the porch could hear the sound of the train's whistle drifting up the cove.

A stay at White Sulphur Springs around the start of the last century represented a dramatic departure from noisy, congested city life where mills and factories belched clouds of coal smoke which often delayed the dawn and brought an early dusk. The change was immediately apparent to the weary traveler upon arriving at the Sulphur Springs station, which was situated deep in a picturesque valley whose hillsides were dotted with dairy farms. After enduring many hours — perhaps even days — aboard a succession of non-air-conditioned trains, guests would gratefully disembark from their sooty coaches. Amidst clouds of steam, trunks and suitcases were hoisted from the baggage car to the ground, as excited children released pent-up energy by running around the little depot or getting acquainted with the team of horses waiting to take them on the final leg of their long journey. The hissing steam locomotive with its little train would soon labor off through the valley toward Huntingdon, Altoona, or Cumberland, the sound of its whistle growing ever-fainter, and the new arrivals would leave behind them thoughts of the city house they had shuttered for the summer, along with the hustle and bustle of Pittsburgh, Chicago, New York, or Philadelphia.

Guests found their tensions continuing to evaporate as they relaxed on the swaying carriage ride up the hill and through the deep woods, the journey punctuated by occasional sunny openings in the canopy of trees. They found themselves enveloped by a silence interrupted only by nature, with Milligan's Cove serving as a home to scarlet tanagers, indigo buntings, wild canaries, cardinals — and, in season, the spectacle of majestic Monarch butterflies. The visitors' reasons for coming to this oasis were many and varied, ranging from the peace and quiet to the fresh air, the good food, or perhaps the hope of finding a cure for a persistent ailment. A half-hour later, they were being warmly greeted at the hotel's front door by the Colvin family. After they signed the large guest register book and shook off the dust of the long train ride, they quickly felt at home. Soon friendships were being renewed or forged, in animated discussions at the dinner table or during quiet conversations on porch rockers which often continued long after darkness had surrounded the cozy, softly lit hotel and the mysterious forests echoed with the soothing sounds of crickets, owls, and tree frogs.

VIEW ON ROAD TO COLVIN'S SULPHUR SPRINGS, PA

Crossing the mountain from Johnstown to White Sulphur Springs, 1895;
on the road to White Sulphur Springs (postcard: 1908)

Accommodations at the hotel were not luxurious. Guest rooms were simply furnished, and the dining room floor was made of plain wide boards. The elegant front staircase likewise had no carpeting, and electricity was not introduced until well into the twentieth century. And yet visitors were satisfied with these relatively modest surroundings, focusing instead on the spectacular natural setting of the resort.

A decade after the Colvins took over ownership, a relative of John P. Reed, the original co-owner of White Sulphur Springs, made a visit to the resort and took away vivid memories: "The location of the hotel to me was charming and pretty, presenting a picturesque appearance, with a dense grove of large and spreading evergreen trees, and near a spring of odorous sulphur water of medicinal value, from which the place derives its name. When I awoke from my slumbers in the morning I found the weather delightful and refreshing, and the air filled with the song of numerous birds; particularly above all others was the plaintive cry of the whip-poor-will. All

A 1930s rate card and an early register book.

NOTICE.

Rates for this room are---

Per day $2.50
For one person . $15.00 per week
For two persons . $22.00 per week

FULL RATES FOR CHILDREN, SAME AS ADULTS
Noisy and Unruly Children Not Tolerated.

Guests leaving will give at least twenty-four hours notice at the office in advance to secure room in the coach.

M. S. COLVIN & CO., Proprietors

this charmed me so that I have never been able to forget the impression made by the night's stay and the visit with the Colvins."

White Sulphur Springs guests were well-fed. In a June 11, 1897, letter to the *Bedford Gazette* editor, "B.M.T." recounted a day spent at the hotel, giving high marks to the dining room. "The hotel is not surpassed anywhere for the quality of the fare and the reasonable price for boarding. The lovers of good, home-made bread, pure butter, fresh eggs, rich milk, etc., can be supplied here to their hearts' content. The ladies of the house are to be commended for their care for appetites and comforts of the guests."

An 1893 guest expressed her approval differently when she wrote to friends back home, "Weighed 97 lbs when I came to Sulphur, gained 4 lbs in 3 wks."

According to a newspaper retrospective about the resort's early days, "Meals — hearty, nourishing meals of Bedford County cooking — were taken at a communal long table with the rest of the guests of the hotel. The

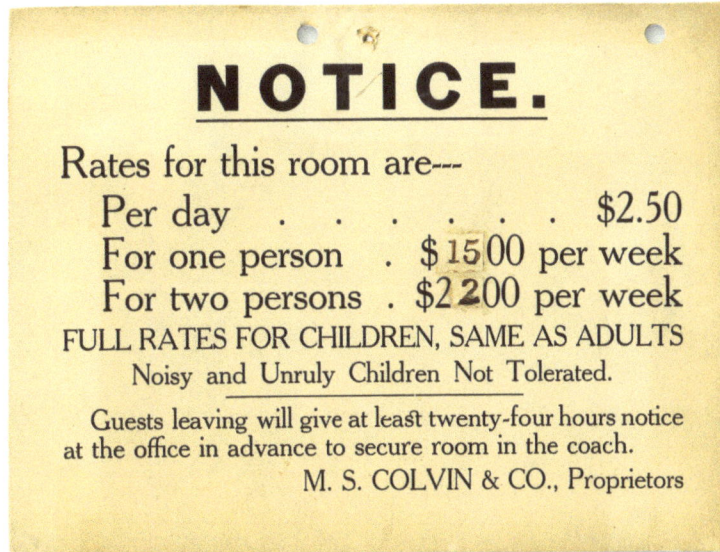

REGISTER   WHITE SULPHUR SPRINGS HOTEL

Some Colvin cousins at White Sulphur Springs, c. 1890

meals were served after the ring of a huge bell, and there was no choice of menu, but the food was wholesome and hot … and no one ever complained of malnutrition as a White Sulphur Springs guest." Tables seated 10 to 12 people, and each guest sat at the same place for each meal throughout his or her stay.

In August 1941, the school bell used to announce mealtime was wielded by Mary Lybarger, who so impressed guest J.F. Record that he gallantly wrote a poem in her honor, "When Mary Rings The Bell." Among its verses:

The health food it is good and the pancakes they are swell.
That's the reason why we rush for breakfast
*   when Mary rings the bell.*

And for supper too we're ready and we sit and sniff and smell.
Wondering what we'll have to eat when Mary rings the bell.

Helen Waugerman Foor, a waitress in the hotel dining room at age 16, still remembered nearly 70 years later the dashing Mr. Record, recalling with a twinkle in her eye that he "drove a blue convertible!"

The hotel's bowling alley building also housed the Sulphur Springs post office (established in 1897) with tri-daily mails and an Adams Express office, as well as the candy and cold drink stand. The Colvin brothers apparently saw potential in businesses supplementing the hotel trade, portraying themselves on White Sulphur Springs stationery as "dealers in Groceries, Confections and Fine Cigars."

Tennis players (1908) and croquet players (1940s)

Starting in the late 1920s, early automobiles could be refueled from an impressive glass-topped Atlantic Gasoline pump situated at the corner of the bowling alley building, across the road from the main hotel.

Outdoor recreational activities at the resort included lawn tennis, hiking, archery, horseshoes, and swimming. On a typical afternoon, athletic guests were all outside engaged in these pursuits, while others were taking naps upstairs or playing checkers on the porch. Many took long, leisurely walks along the lightly traveled country roads. At dinnertime, guests brought from their rooms water pitchers which they placed in the front hall on a small walnut table covered with white oilcloth. They left them there until they were ready to go to bed, when they went down to the spring and filled the pitchers to take back to their rooms. With limited indoor plumbing, this practice of guests carrying their own drinking water apparently continued into the 1940s. A former employee confided that the secret to enjoying the spring water was to "let it sit" overnight, after which its strong sulphur aroma had dissipated.

The spring house from which guests drew water (1950s) and the spring house with Big Mike (1920s).

One prominent natural feature of the resort was "Big Mike," a massive white pine tree named for Michael Colvin. Thought to be at least 300 years old, it was considered the tallest tree in Bedford County. With an estimated height of 158 feet, it towered over the hotel from its location just to the north, near the spring pavilion, and it was featured in a series of early hotel picture postcards. (The legendary tree was carefully nurtured by the Cochrans into the 1960s until its final remnant fell victim to lightning strikes and decay.)

Patricia Cochran had especially fond memories from childhood of certain informal Colvin hotel traditions.

"Just off the porch over at the big building," she reminisced, "they had three pieces of wood in the ground against the porch to make a square. And when you would get awake in the morning, you would hear 'thump, thump, thump' and you'd know, 'Ah, it's ice cream day.' They were breaking up the ice in that little square, getting

ready for the ice cream. They had a hoe handle inside the end of a small log to break up the ice. And they always had plain ice cream and another ice cream with fruit that was in season…peaches, strawberries, whatever."

The Colvin family style of hotel ownership and management was reflected in the cordial, familiar tone of

ROBERT L. PIPER, M. D.
1251 LOGAN AVENUE
TYRONE, PA.

June 25 1927.

Colvin's White Sulphur Springs,
Bedford County,
Pa.

Friend Colvin:

        Can you reserve two adjoining rooms for me for
a week or ten days beginning August 21? Roasting ears and
chickens should be nice and ripe just about that time. Horseshoe pitching should be in full blast and the sulphur water as
good as ever.

        Hoping to see you at that time, I am

                                Very truly yours,

                                R. L. PIPER M. D.

correspondence from guests, many of whom returned to the resort year after year and some of whom requested guest rooms by number or location. A file from 1927 contains letters addressed to "Dear Mr. Mike," "Friend Colvin," and "My Very Dear Mike," with several also inquiring about the health of Michael's family.

A frequent guest from Washington, Pennsylvania wrote: "August 9, 1927. My Dear Mr. Colvin: It is getting on toward the time of going to Sulphur Springs. I am planning to go the day after Labor Day Sept. 6th if all goes well. And if I can have my old room no. 19 will be very much obliged to you. I have been having a rather strenuous summer of it & will be most thankful for a good rest,

such as I always have at S.S. Please remember me to Mrs. Colvin and your sisters."

Like the regular hotel guests, former employee Helen Foor retained fond memories of the Colvins, calling them "good, solid folks." Michael Colvin, she said, was "a staunch Republican, naturally sophisticated and somewhat reserved—I was a bit intimidated by him." Mrs. Colvin was "such a lady…a lovely person…fair, down-to-earth, and approachable…small and appearing frail although she was really quite strong." Mrs. Foor considered working as a housekeeper for the Colvins a wonderful learning experience. Decades later, she was still influenced by Mrs. Colvin's instruction that, after she finished cleaning a room, she should always ask herself, "Did I miss anything?" Her total pay at the end of a summer of 12-hour, 7 a.m.–7 p.m. days: $55.

Some visitors to the resort had more than relaxation in mind. The curative reputation of sulphur waters prompted sufferers of various ailments and conditions to contact the Colvins, holding out hope that a stay at White Sulphur Springs would bring them relief or perhaps a cure. In 1927, the president of a Pittsburgh door and sash company wrote, after reading a testimonial published by the hotel, "I notice the letter from Dr. Endfield mentions amongst other ailments for which your Sulphur Baths should be used is paralysis. I suffered from a stroke two years last July, my right side being affected … leaving me very little control in walking or in the movement of my arm. Can you advise me what would be the probable effect of your Hot Sulphur Baths? Awaiting the favor of your reply …."

The Colvins were not reluctant to promote the benefits of the spring waters. A 1920s pamphlet proclaimed: "It is one of Nature's best known remedies for all Liver, Kidney and Stomach Troubles, Gravel, Gall Stones, Jaundice, Diabetes, Rheumatism and Gout."

A curious health-related sidelight was an item published in an April 16, 1920, Bedford newspaper announcing, "White Sulphur Springs Hotel Sold to Company of Pittsburgh Physicians." The article stated that the Colvins had sold the hotel and 130 surrounding acres for "upwards of $50,000" to a Dr. W.W. Thompson of Pitcairn, Pennsylvania, and that "… the new owners plan to use the hotel building as a sanitarium with Dr. Thompson the resident physician in charge." Nothing further was ever reported about the supposed transaction, and White Sulphur Springs continued as a Colvin-owned resort into the 1940s. It is interesting to note, however, that several years before the announcement, in an era of tuberculosis resorts and "cure cottages," the Pennsylvania state legislature had appropriated significant monies " … for the establishment of free sanitariums to be located in forest locations … where the poor may be cared for." It is possible that the Colvins, with no heirs to potentially take over the business, may

WHITE SULPHUR SPRINGS HOTEL
Heated Throughout by a Most Modern Hot Water System

A BEAUTIFUL RETREAT AMONG THE PINES AND MOUNTAINS OF BEDFORD COUNTY, PA. A LARGE THREE-STORY HOTEL WITH BROAD VERANDAS SURROUNDING THE SAME.

M. S. COLVIN & CO.

THE SULPHUR AND IRON WATER COMBINED IS UNSURPASSED. TERMS FROM $15 TO $21 PER WEEK; $2.50 TO $3.50 PER DAY. OPEN EARLY AND LATE IN THE SEASON.

SANITARY PLUMBING—HOT AND COLD SULPHUR BATHS

Sulphur Springs, Bedford Co., Pa.,_____193__

THE HOT SULPHUR BATHS.

Appreciating the great benefit accruing from sulphur baths—hot and cold, as the case may require, we have just installed a complete system of water works, supplying the hotel and baths with the sulphur water from the springs. This supply is so abundant that fire protection and all sanitary demands are met.

The advantage of bathing in this wonderful water, filled with the sulphur gases of the spring, cannot be overestimated. For years physicians have urged us to install these baths, but the cost was heavy and we hesitated until the ever-increasing popularity of this resort warranted the large investment. This is particularly true of the hot baths. Physician after physician has insisted upon the use of the water for their patients. Now they have a pure and copious supply heated in air tight coils, and never exposed to the air until it is drawn into the bath.

As a recuperative agent the water in connection with pine-laden air and restful conditions of its environments, is unequaled, and in kidney and bladder troubles, dyspepsia, jaundice and skin disorders, it is almost a specific cure and has been known as such for one hundred years.

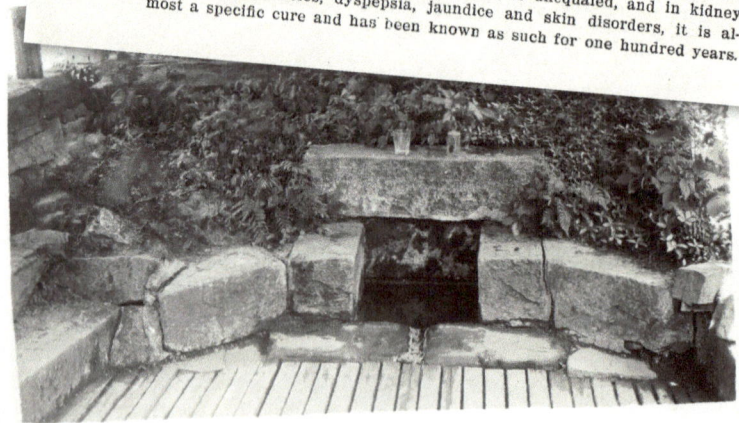

A page of 1930s stationery, a page from a c. 1900 promotional brochure, and a postcard of the sulphur spring.

have briefly considered selling when an attractive offer was presented. Michael and Lorena's first son had died the day of birth, their second son had died in 1919 at the age of 3, and the sisters, all unmarried, were either in or approaching retirement. Former hotel co-owner Ross Colvin's only son had been born after his father had left the family business; unlike his aunts and uncles, he had not grown up with exposure to the hotel business, and his future career would lie elsewhere.

In the early years of Colvin management, White Sulphur Springs drew its patronage primarily from central Pennsylvania and the Cumberland, Maryland, area, with fewer but still significant numbers of guests journeying from Philadelphia, Pittsburgh, Baltimore, Washington, D.C., and New York City. At the time, travel to the hotel by rail, even within the state, often involved an entire day, with one or more connections en route. Some guests came much longer distances, many of these from midwestern cities. Hotel registers show repeat visitors from St. Louis, Kansas City, Chicago, and central Indiana, and as the years went by, the automobile clearly had a broadening geographical effect on the clientele base.

Among the regular guests were members of the J. Harvey Patterson family. On June 14, 1910, Mrs. Patterson and her five-year-old daughter Patricia (later Patricia Cochran) registered at White Sulphur Springs for a month-long stay, introducing the child to the resort she and her husband would one day own. The year before the Pattersons' visit, a cousin of Patricia brought to the hotel another cousin, Lorena Smelker, who would become Mrs. Michael Colvin.

From an early age, Patricia began to gather mental images of the members of the Colvin family members she came to know over the next several decades.

"I remember Michael Colvin with great fondness," she said. "He was truly a great Christian gentleman, one of the pillars of the Presbyterian Church in Schellsburg and

A young Patricia Patterson with her mother, around the time of her first visit to White Sulphur Springs.

so good to me as a youngster. He had a Ford pickup truck that he parked in the driveway, and the poor man could never get out of the drive to go on an errand that I wasn't in that truck. He would take me everyplace, which was very kind."

Michael Colvin once admitted to a friend that he had never really wanted to own a hotel but stayed with the business to help his sisters earn a living. As a result, he persevered in operating White Sulphur Springs through the remainder of his life, in much the same way that the Cochrans, also reluctant innkeepers, would later devote three decades to keeping the hotel open, despite many challenges.

A generally quiet and soft-spoken man, even Michael Colvin had his breaking point, and he apparently reached it one morning over the hotel's telephone service, which was on a party line accessed via a single hand-crank phone on the wall in the office. According to a guest, Mr. Colvin had been trying to place a business call but was blocked by a mother and her daughter who both resided nearby. Clearly not familiar with using the telephone, they were discussing at length the beans the mother was serving for dinner and the fact that the daughter was hanging her wash on the clothesline. Finally, Mr. Colvin could take the situation no longer. He picked up the phone and exclaimed, "Mrs. Jones, your beans are burning!" The mother cried, "Oh my goodness!" and immediately hung up.

"Mrs. Colvin was a marvelous cook," Mrs. Cochran recalled. "She would turn out very delectable pastries. She was a delightful woman…a great deal of charm. As a small child, I loved her."

Despite its sheltered location, the cove was sometimes buffeted by violent weather, and on one occasion, Lorena Colvin was entertaining a friend in the kitchen of the cottage next to the hotel during a severe electrical storm.

Michael S. Colvin, c. 1930s.

"Mrs. Colvin had a little white towel covering the radiator right alongside of where I was sitting. We got up and went into the dining room and sat down, and just as we did there was a terrific explosion and a flash of light in the kitchen. Of course we could smell the electricity. And alongside where I had been sitting, the little white towel had a black hole in it about as big as a quarter. Lightning had struck the radiator."

Guest registers indicate that business at the hotel probably peaked between 1905 and 1915, then leveled off and remained fairly constant until the mid-1930s. In 1912, a room assignment ledger showed the overwhelmed Colvins assigning guests to the three second-floor guest rooms and sleeping porch in the next-door cottage; a hallway; a parlor; a tiny guest room on the second floor of the bowling alley building; and "BROK" (Back Room Over Kitchen). Although Abraham May's Mountain House and Hezekiah May's Arlington Cottage Hotel were no longer actively seeking guests by the mid-1890s, White Sulphur Springs register notes indicate that May family members residing in the area — Abraham's widow Sarah and her son Albert, and possibly also Hezekiah — were hosting occasional overflow boarders from the hotel as late as 1913.

Michael Colvin expanded White Sulphur Springs' land

holdings in Milligan's Cove in 1928 when he purchased two adjoining parcels totaling approximately 40 acres from neighbors B.F. Madore and Jo. W. Tate for $800. The property, located to the southwest of the hotel building, had been owned by Hezekiah May, proprietor of the early Arlington Cottage Hotel. Following Hezekiah's death, four tracts totaling 475 acres were acquired by lumberman Tate who, in turn, sold a half-interest to Madore in February 1928. Michael bought the 40 acres on June 9 of that year. The acquisition was important to the resort because the northern boundary of the property came within a few yards of the hotel building, and the added acreage now provided a buffer against future outside development as well as new land for trails and other recreational uses. The Colvin land holdings were largely completed in April 1931 when Amanda Wertz sold Michael, for $35, a one-acre tract close to the hotel which had been isolated in the center of Colvin-owned land by the Madore-Tate purchase. White Sulphur Springs encompassed a total of approximately 140 acres for the next 20 years.

The gathering clouds of World War II, with its restrictions on travel and following as it did the lean years of the Great Depression, led to a downturn in business at White Sulphur Springs which gradually grew more pronounced. Henry Ford's Model T and Model A had given Americans a degree of mobility they had never known, and roads like the Pennsylvania Turnpike enabled travelers to bypass the once-obligatory and much more leisurely route through Bedford and other Lincoln Highway towns. The need for overflow accommodations had long since passed, and the Colvins now occupied both floors of the cottage next to the hotel.

The automobile also led to the demise of railroad travel to White Sulphur Springs. A desk clerk noted in the hotel register on August 14, 1903, the arrival of the "First Automobile at S.S." The second auto did not arrive until

November 3, 1906, but it was not long before cars were commonplace.

Passenger service to the little Sulphur Springs station ended on April 24, 1937, although it was possible to travel by rail to nearby Mann's Choice and Buffalo Mills until September 25 of the same year. The abandoned Sulphur Springs depot reportedly was moved to Buffalo Mills and converted into a private residence which was demolished some years later. (Until November 1953, the Huntingdon & Broad Top Mountain Railroad still brought a few passengers to Bedford from the Pennsylvania Railroad in Huntingdon.) The Sulphur Springs post office had closed in 1935.

Ross Colvin, long removed from hotel management, passed away in November 1923, and the last of Michael Colvin's siblings, sister Ella, died in 1940 at the age of 76. White Sulphur Springs, its business faltering, reopened for the season in the spring of 1941 and registered its final guest on November 2 of that year. On April 18, 1942, Michael Colvin died, and his widow Lorena, with no family members left to help run the business and gas rationing on the horizon, decided not to reopen in 1942. Most of the hotel's contents were then sold, and the resort's future appeared bleak.

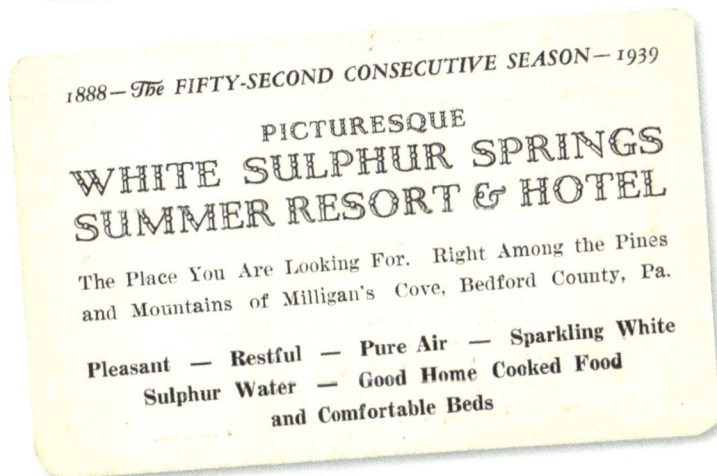

1888 — The FIFTY-SECOND CONSECUTIVE SEASON — 1939

PICTURESQUE

WHITE SULPHUR SPRINGS
SUMMER RESORT & HOTEL

The Place You Are Looking For. Right Among the Pines and Mountains of Milligan's Cove, Bedford County, Pa.

Pleasant — Restful — Pure Air — Sparkling White Sulphur Water — Good Home Cooked Food and Comfortable Beds

The Cochrans Become Stewards of White Sulphur Springs

The players seemed ill-suited for the task — two Midwestern big-city people, one a successful manufacturer of heavy construction machinery and the other a celebrated artist from Chicago's Gold Coast, both giving up their former lives and investing their life savings to come to the rescue of a derelict country inn in rural Pennsylvania.

Paul and Patricia Cochran had no previous experience in the hospitality industry when they took on the most formidable task either had ever faced. Nevertheless, their unlikely White Sulphur Springs ownership scenario endured for 32 years, although the Cochrans would both later admit that the challenges exceeded anything they had expected. What began as a hobby soon turned into a year-round commitment that was to test their resolve time and time again.

Paul Briggs Cochran was born in 1898 in Peru, Indiana. After attending high school in Springfield, Missouri, he studied for two years at the University of Arkansas, worked in the booming Oklahoma oil fields, and then enrolled in the University of Minnesota before enlisting in the U.S. Army. There he served in the 351st Infantry (88th Division) in France and was honorably discharged as a 2nd Lieutenant in 1919, receiving his bachelor's degree from the University of Minnesota the following year. After selling Stearns-Knight and Auburn automobiles in Minneapolis in the early 1920s, Paul got his start in the construction industry working with his older brother, with one project involving the use of inmates from the state penitentiary to build modern concrete highways in Michigan. He then secured a job as a salesman of heavy equipment, traveling throughout the eastern United States as well as to Europe and the Caribbean, including Cuba. In 1930, the year before he and Patricia were married, he formed his own construction machinery and supply business in Chicago, and

over the next 20 years he managed and owned a variety of construction-related equipment firms, eventually becoming the general manager of the Buckeye Traction Ditcher Co. of Findlay, Ohio. Buckeye's products included the R-B Power Finegrader used extensively in roadbed grading for highway projects, among them the first sections of the Pennsylvania Turnpike. During World War II, the firm manufactured construction equipment for the Army, earning Buckeye the coveted Army-Navy "E" Production Award in 1944 from the Secretary of War for high achievement in producing materiel needed for the war effort.

In 1945, Cochran co-founded the Tractomotive Corporation, which was the first company in the industry

19-year-old Paul Cochran in 1917.

to design and build shovels and other attachments for heavy-duty crawlers and rubber-tired tractors, and also produced bulldozers, snow plows, and related items for military troop carriers and tanks. Two years later, while still associated with Tractomotive, he took on his most ambitious project yet—the restoration and reopening of White Sulphur Springs.

Patricia Lucille Patterson was born in 1904 in Pittsburgh to the former Birdella Sarah Morgan, a native of Clearfield, Pennsylvania; and J. Harvey Patterson from nearby Berwinsdale. J. Harvey's 40-year career in the insurance business saw him named to senior executive positions with a succession of major companies. The job changes, together with the fragile health of his wife, often prompted long moves for his family. In later years, Patricia Cochran always credited her father with teaching her the athletic skills that made her the equal of male competitors. She learned to play tennis, shoot, fence, swim, and ride, and her father had small golf clubs made so that she could join him on the course. In the process, she acquired a degree of independence which would enable her to take on the White Sulphur Springs project with her husband four decades later.

A botched blind date in the late 1920s resulted in the first meeting between Patricia and Paul. Friends had originally set her up with a young man traveling to Chicago from out of town. When he canceled at the last minute, Paul agreed to substitute as a favor. On their third date, Paul proposed marriage. With a stubborn streak as pronounced as his, she initially resisted, but two years later she gave in. They were married on July 8, 1931, at St. Luke's Church, Evanston, Illinois, and settled into a stylish, church-owned apartment at 425 Grove Street, Evanston. Eventually, they also purchased a house in Findlay, Ohio, at 913 South Main Street, not far from the Buckeye Traction Ditcher plant.

Patricia Patterson's first visit with her mother to White Sulphur Springs in June and July of 1910 was followed by another later that year, a relatively short trip from their home near Philadelphia. In 1913, the family having relocated to California because of Birdella Patterson's health, mother and daughter returned to the hotel via the Santa Fe Railroad's "California Limited" and the Pennsylvania Railroad. Those early vacations left strong impressions on Patricia, who recalled her delight at building little log cabins out of twigs beneath the sweeping pine trees. From these initial visits, a photograph survives of a wide-eyed Patricia seated in the crook of a tree, clearly enthralled by the natural beauty surrounding her.

Beginning in 1919 when the Pattersons were again living on the East Coast, Patricia and her parents were regular guests at White Sulphur Springs, with their stays lasting up to a month. Patricia, an aspiring artist, pursued her interest in drawing and painting at Beaver College near Philadelphia. She later attended Chicago's Academy of Fine Arts and Art Institute after her family relocated to the Chicago area in the 1920s, and she was a pupil of English artist Frederic Victor Poole. After her marriage, she studied with portrait artist Robert Brackman at his studio in New London, Connecticut, and her paintings were displayed at Chicago-area juried exhibitions. Her husband was fully supportive of these artistic endeavors, demonstrating the same devotion to his wife which later prompted him to fulfill her wish by purchasing White Sulphur Springs.

"By the time I began coming to White Sulphur Springs," Patricia recalled of her visits as an adult in the 1920s and '30s, "the automobile was already changing the entire resort business. Formerly, guests took big trunks and stayed longer because life was different then. When I was here as a guest, people would come and stay a week, two weeks, maybe a month at most."

Patricia introduced her fiancé to White Sulphur Springs early in their engagement, and the couple made regular visits there throughout the 1930s, some trips likely coinciding with Paul's extensive Pennsylvania Turnpike equipment dealings. Patricia and her mother would spend several weeks at the resort, with Paul faithfully stopping in for weekend stays, traveling from Chicago or wherever else his business had taken him.

Helen Foor, who worked for the Colvins and later for the Cochrans, remembered Patricia in 1941 as "beautiful...nice and kind. She had a presence about her. She turned heads but wasn't spoiled—her mother Birdella wouldn't spoil her. She always greeted everyone

16-year-old Patricia Patterson in 1920;
Michael Colvin and Patricia at the hotel, 1930s.

by their first name. We were always glad to see the Cochrans and Pattersons."

The Cochrans remained close to the Colvins through the years, and so it was not surprising that Patricia was deeply distressed by the hotel's closure and by potential buyers who would have ruined the beauty of the property. They visited White Sulphur Springs more frequently and checked into the hotel as guests for the last time in August 1941, eight months before Michael Colvin's death. After his passing, Lorena Colvin made the decision to shutter the resort but continued to live in the cottage next to the closed hotel.

"For years after Mr. Colvin died," Patricia recalled, "the hotel stood empty, a great big black place at night with no lights. There was almost nothing in it because Mrs. Colvin had sold everything when he died. And it remained empty until the latter part of 1946, when Mrs. Colvin had decided she was going to sell it to a lumber man who was going to come in and lumber all these virgin trees."

The Cochrans were a devoted couple with strong religious faith. (Answering a neighbor's question about his belief in the Lord, Paul Cochran replied simply, "I've been too near death too many times not to be saved.") After prayer and deliberation, they finally made the decision that they could not stand by and see White Sulphur Springs destroyed. In September 1946, a Bedford newspaper reported that Lorena Colvin had sold the White Sulphur Springs resort and 140 acres of land to Paul Cochran, and thus began the Cochrans' stewardship that would continue until 1978.

Mrs. Cochran explained, "We didn't want to see the trees go, because when the trees went, the spring would go, and the spring has a very marvelous quality. So we

The cottage next to the hotel, 1950.

bought it to save the trees, never intending to go into the hotel business. We found that the locust posts which were supporting the hotel were swinging in the breeze. We didn't know what was holding up the hotel unless it was its past reputation. So we started in to save the building, and the first thing we knew, we woke up and found ourselves in the hotel business."

Another consideration that probably influenced the Cochrans' decision was the fact that Patricia Patterson Cochran had a family tie, albeit a distant one, with Lorena Smelker Colvin and thus with the family which had overseen White Sulphur Springs since its second year of operation. Mrs. Cochran's maternal great-grandmother was a member of the Smelker family, and there may have been a connection between the first trip by Birdella Patterson and her daughter Patricia to White Sulphur Springs in 1910—and a 1909 visit by Lorena Smelker to the resort, where she met and charmed the man who would become her husband, Michael Colvin. When Lorena Colvin wrote to Paul Cochran in 1946 on the occasion of the ownership change, she told him how pleased she was "… that you are the new owners and that this property stays in the family, not going to the hands of strangers as would eventually have happened since I could not have kept it always."

As part of her agreement with the Cochrans, Lorena reserved the right to occupy the cottage rent-free for the rest of her life and to have free use of land for her vegetable garden as well as access to the hotel garage for her car. Lorena remained in the cottage until, a year after the Cochrans reopened White Sulphur Springs, she asked Paul if she might be able to move into the main building. A suite was readied for her, and she made it her residence, with the Cochrans and their hotel staff looking after her, until her death in May 1961. The cottage was converted into storage, mainly for furniture from the Cochrans' Chicago and Findlay homes which would not fit into their own suite in the hotel.

Virginia Lankey, who was sometimes assigned to deliver food to the cottage while employed as a hotel waitress in the late 1940s and early '50s, recalled that Mrs. Colvin was "a very nice lady. We all liked her." Mrs. Colvin was always appreciative of the staff's efforts on her behalf, Virginia said, and she would regularly set out pieces of her personal china from which employees could select "thank-you" gifts. Today, Virginia treasures several of these mementos, as well as an elaborate dress knitted by Mrs. Colvin especially for Virginia's doll.

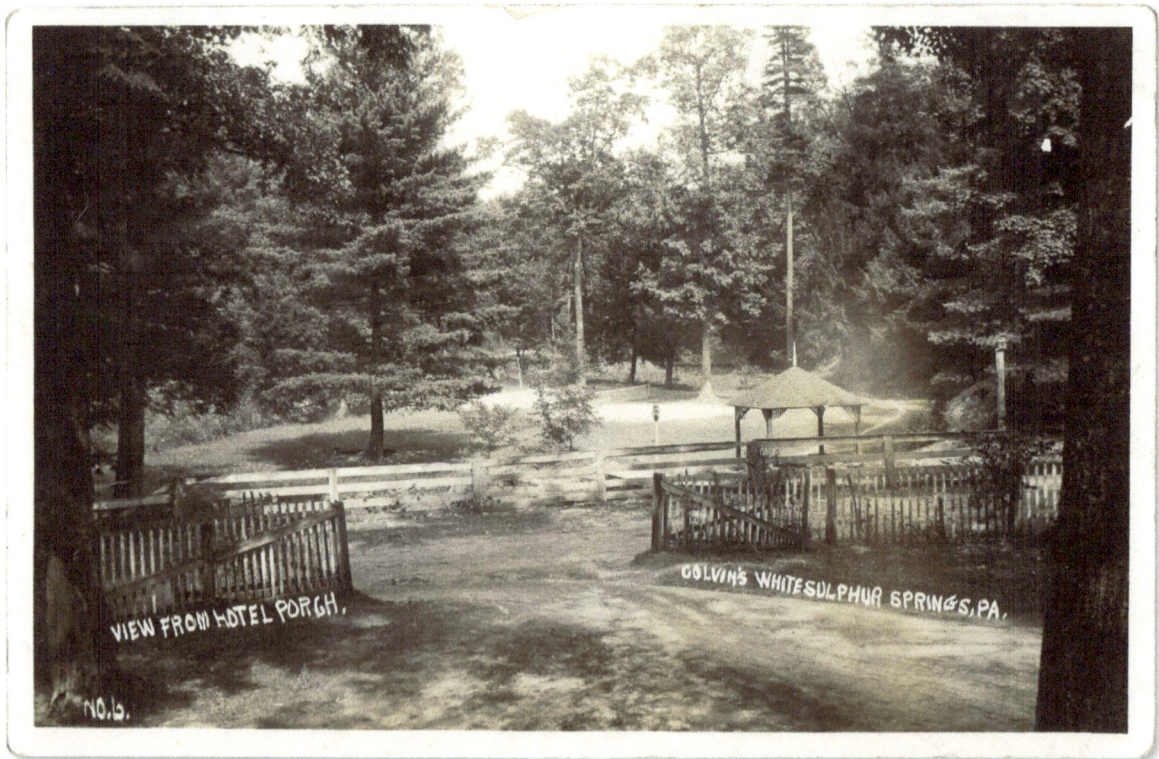

The view from the hotel porch (1911 postcard)

Rebuilding a Pennsylvania Landmark

A sympathetic observer of their effort to reopen White Sulphur Springs wrote, "The Cochrans had more sentiment than sense, more courage than business caution, and a disarming lack of knowledge of the resort business that led them to try to recreate the gracious life of the 1900s in a modern, comfortable setting. Clearly they were more at home in Chicago's Drake Hotel than in a tiny mountain hamlet that you can't even find on most maps." (*Hillcrest* [Ohio] *Sun-Press*, May 19, 1955)

And yet the interests, skills, and independent spirit of the couple proved equal to the challenge, particularly in the renovation process. Patricia Cochran demonstrated her artistic flair as she plunged into the task of interior decorating, while her husband took over management of the grounds, planting thousands of new pines and pink dogwoods to blend with the natural white dogwoods covering the mountain crests.

Paul Cochran inspects the man-made fishing pond behind the hotel (1950s).

The Cochrans, in planning to reopen White Sulphur Springs, were well-aware that the day was past when hotel guests could be expected to rough it, even in such a remote area as Milligan's Cove. Finding that they had to rebuild the hotel from the inside out, they remained committed to perpetuating its original appearance and function, with the goal of operating "a true country inn," as Paul described it. The *Bedford Gazette* reported that the Cochrans' approach was "one of preservation of the natural beauty and restoration of the physical property to an extent of modernization for the physical comforts, but without jeopardizing or destroying any of the natural advantages and beauty of the area." Paul insisted on retaining the White Sulphur Springs Hotel name, rather than formally calling it an inn or a spa, to sustain the continuity of the designation which, according to local legend, dated back to the log hotel of the 1700s.

Of course, the enduring centerpiece of the resort was the sulphur spring, which the Cochrans improved by replacing decayed wood sides with cement beneath the rebuilt pavilion. The spring's waters were promoted, in hotel advertising, for healthy vacationers, convalescents, and the chronically ill: "The therapeutic advantages of the Spring's moderately mineralized water and a complete change of climate, especially in such attractive surroundings, makes a vacation at White Sulphur Springs one of true rehabilitation." In *The Vanishing Spas of Pennsylvania (An Historical Review)*, Drs. Igho Kornblueh and Geo. Morris Piersol noted additional restorative advantages of the resort, located 1,200 feet above sea level: "Convalescents, hypertensives, and persons with chronic heart disease in a stage of full compensation, will find White Sulphur Springs a restful place, with level walks and the environment helpful in the management of such conditions." Patricia Cochran claimed that several of her friends obtained relief from severe arthritis after drinking the water, and in the late 20th century it was still commonplace to see area residents filling their containers at the spring pavilion.

Over a six-year period starting in 1947, the Cochrans invested $150,000 in renovating and restoring the hotel, living temporarily at the Fort Bedford Inn in downtown Bedford during frequent visits from their homes in Chicago and Ohio. The addition of some fire escapes represented the principal visible exterior alteration to the main hotel building, but renovations inside it and the various other structures were much more extensive. To make the necessary changes, they drew upon expertise found locally and in distant cities. The rebuilding project provided steady employment for approximately 20 area residents, including five women who were assigned to sewing rooms in the hotel to make draperies and bedspreads. Near the site of the old log hotel, the Cochrans erected a barn for their flock of Shropshire sheep whose wool was used to make blankets for the hotel.

An advertisement in the June 27, 1950, *Bedford Inquirer* placed by Albert Pick and Company of Chicago boasted, "We are happy to have been selected to provide your ultramodern kitchen, dining room equipment and bedroom carpets." In a list of the hotel's many features,

the Cochrans pointed out, "Two kitchens are arranged, one in back of the other, so that no cooking odors may penetrate the dining room." In a separate building constructed to blend in with its surroundings, the Creamery Package Manufacturing Company of Chicago installed a deep freeze cold storage plant, with blue light to kill bacteria and a trolley running through three rooms to age meat scientifically. Bedroom furniture for the hotel was delivered by the William P. Taylor Company of New York, and Demmler & Schenck of Pittsburgh arranged for Shenango China bearing the distinctive green White Sulphur Springs monogram.

Mrs. Cochran could often be found in work clothes exploring the construction, and she delighted in engaging in friendly target practice with the laborers, using a revolver, during lunchtime competition.

"The men used to call me 'Annie Oakley'," she remembered with a smile.

The south end of the hotel (1950s)

THE GRAND REOPENING

Finally, on July 1, 1950, eight years after many thought its doors had closed forever, the White Sulphur Springs Hotel was formally reopened to great fanfare, although it would be 1955 before all improvements were completed. A pre-opening buffet supper was scheduled as a gesture of appreciation to the families of workers who renovated the building, and local newspapers covered the proceedings extensively, welcoming back a resort which, for decades, had meant so much to visitors from afar and area residents alike. Guests were relieved to find that required improvements did not compromise the traditional ambiance. In an effort to recreate an atmosphere of Colonial times, the Cochrans decorated the first-floor parlors with period and regional antiques, including some original hotel pieces which they had purchased from the Colvin family and, in the formal parlor, a Steinway grand piano. Paintings, many of them executed by Mrs. Cochran and depicting scenes around the property, occupied the walls. A parlor case displayed treasures of Milligan's Cove, including earthenware, American Indian crafts, ceramics, and muskets, as well as several bayonets said to have been found within the hotel's original walls. The dining room, able to accommodate up to 125 guests, featured 10 framed portraits of Indian chiefs contributed by Dr. John Bowman, ex-chancellor of the University of Pittsburgh and a close friend of the Cochrans.

The *Bedford Inquirer*'s account of the reopening noted that "the guest rooms have been redone in pleasing pastel shades, with a motif of forest green setting the style. The bedroom furniture is all in colonial maple, rubbed to an almost honey-colored finish. The decorating of the guest quarters has been carefully supervised by Mrs. Paul Cochran. The last word in modern bathroom equipment has been added." Six old beds with matching dressers and

Billboard, entrance hall, and parlor from the 1950s.

A 1956 promotional map; an early advertising brochure; and the first rate card from 1950.

tables had been left in the building by Mrs. Colvin, and these golden oak pieces were refinished and put back into service.

The guest accommodations in the main building had been reconfigured into 46 bedrooms (four on the first floor, 20 on the second, and 22 on the third), each with a private or connecting bath, a change that necessitated the installation of 26 bathrooms. The modifications, including the conversion of three first-floor bedrooms into a second parlor, reduced total lodging capacity, which suited the Cochrans' management style as emphasized in their first advertising brochure: "You will find at the White Sulphur Springs Inn a truly friendly, informal, intimate atmosphere since we limit the guest total to about eighty persons." Daily rates in the early 1950s were $11 for a single room and $22.50 for a double, including all meals. Reservations could be made via the hotel's telephone number — Bedford 848.

Although sulphur baths in spring water piped into the hotel were at first offered — on the second floor in the middle wing, staffed by a masseuse — two years after reopening, the Cochrans decided to close their bath department because space was needed for guest rooms and the feature was seldom used. Into the late 1960s, however, sulphur water was still available in one suite on the first floor and another on the second floor, with independent hot water heaters installed for sulphur baths in each. Other changes included removal of a barber shop which the Colvins had maintained in the rear of the first floor. The Cochrans also decided not to reactivate the Sulphur Springs post office or the candy/soft drink counter which had been located in the bowling alley. Otherwise, guests who had not been to the hotel since the Colvins' ownership found things very much as they remembered.

The Cochrans purchased several adjoining parcels of land in 1950, 1951, and 1963, and the 140 acres acquired from Lorena Colvin eventually grew to 630. As a result, the new owners sought to expand White Sulphur Springs' appeal to outdoor enthusiasts with a variety of added attractions, which they described in a half-page ad in the *Bedford Inquirer*. Features included a one-acre artificial lagoon-like swimming lake of "cool mountain water" lined with native stone, located "a pleasant woodland walk from the hotel" and created by damming up a small stream above the hotel and building on the foundation of a much older dam. Dr. Bowman had given the Cochrans four old millstones once used as ballast in French ships coming to America. Two of these still serve today as tables situated by the lake.

Fishing was available in nearby trout streams or in a second lake on the property. Slightly under an acre in size, the pond was located 1,500 feet from the main building and stocked with black bass and bluegill. The water supply was also enhanced with an artesian well "with good natural flow," which drillers struck in 1950 at a depth of only 47 feet. Trap and skeet shooting, as well as hunting for deer and small game, was offered in more remote portions of the resort; an archery range was created; a new clay tennis court was built directly across the road from the hotel building; and croquet, shuffleboard, badminton, horseshoe pitching, and "dancing, both round and square" were also advertised. Horseback riding was featured for the first time, using the hotel's "own saddle horses, easy to handle and sure-footed on mountainous terrain." The Cochrans provided five horses for guests and also brought four from Findlay for their personal use, reflecting Patricia's lifelong equestrian interest. Paul Cochran supervised the clearing of seven miles of bridle and nature paths cut throughout the hotel property, using a man, a horse, and a dragline in order to minimize disturbance to the natural environment. For golfers, a short-hole green was provided "for developing iron and putting games," with a full 18-hole course available nearby in Bedford. Hikers found that a climb up Buffalo Mountain was a suitable preparation for the substantial meals served at the hotel.

Attractive gardens were planted. Along the hotel drive were moss roses given to Patricia Cochran by Flora Colvin, a great-granddaughter of George Colvin, transplanted when the farm where Miss Colvin resided and which had been the home of Reuben Colvin and Margaret Reed (parents of Ross and Michael Colvin) was acquired for a state park.

The Cochrans with their horses.

For those seeking indoor entertainment, the Cochrans had dug out the hotel cellar and laid new foundation walls and pillars, creating a soundproof, 2,500-square-foot basement Big Room so that "those who enjoy lively music and perhaps a late game of bridge or other amusements can do so without disturbing those who wish to retire early." The room featured a huge open fieldstone fireplace capable of handling four-foot logs "…that brings the warmth of a crackling fire to every corner of the room," ping pong, shuffleboard, and, for dancing, a piano and an "electric record-changer" playing the latest 78 rpm records. The colorful 1948 AMI brand jukebox had been obtained from a Chicago warehouse which, the Cochrans were later shocked to learn, was a former Al Capone organization enterprise.

Notably not included in the renovation, and never subsequently added in the hotel building: air conditioning (nature generally obliged with a pleasant breeze); direct-dial phones (the Cochrans did replace the single hand-crank hotel telephone with a small plug-in switchboard that connected all rooms); televisions; or a passenger elevator (a primitive, hand-operated baggage "lift" was removed when inspectors found prior to the reopening that it needed a new hoisting cable). The prevailing concept continued to be provision of a suitable place and atmosphere for families and groups wishing "to get away from it all."

A major element of the hotel's renovation, completed somewhat after the reopening, was a separate two-story building designed to emulate "a typical old Pennsylvania log house" and intended as a place for social gatherings and business meetings. Originally called the "Cabin Club House" by the Cochrans and later named "Fort Cochran" by Officers' Christian Fellowship, the new structure was positioned in a clearing at the foot of a mountain ridge, about 100 yards from the hotel on the one-acre piece of land Michael Colvin had purchased from Amanda Wertz in 1931. The building was literally one of a kind — a throwback to construction methods which technology had long superseded. Hand-hewn logs, 48 feet in length,

rose from a 30-inch stone base and were joined without nails and chinked in log cabin fashion. The supporting 12-by-12 cross beams bore the marks of broad and double-bit axes wielded by construction crew members Lawson and Wingard May, grandsons of early Arlington Cottage Hotel boarding house proprietor Hezekiah May. The massive logs were dragged to and moved about the site by horses sometimes guided by Paul Cochran. The entry steps to the building were made of hand-hewn blocks, invisibly joined, and the structure was topped off with a roof of cedar shakes from Portland, Oregon. Inside, the rustic decorations included chandeliers made from the rims of the 200-year-old French mill stones contributed by Dr. Bowman.

And once again the quaint, two-lane bowling alley, thought to have been the first in western Pennsylvania and now one of the oldest in the entire nation, echoed to the tumbling of heavy wooden pins. The Cochrans made only one change in this recreational feature, extending the alleys to regulation length.

The "Big Room;" Patricia Cochran with May brothers Wingard and Lawson during construction of the Cabin Club House (1952), the House exterior and interior; bowlers.

According to Mrs. Cochran, only three small structures of the resort's original buildings are no longer standing — a wash house; a coal house for the cottage next to the hotel; and, attached to the coal house, a small barn-like structure that served as an ice storage house.

While many local residents found permanent jobs at White Sulphur Springs when it reopened for business, the Cochrans went farther afield to fill certain key positions. The former catering manager at Chicago's posh Drake Hotel, Alphonse Zappelloni, was retained to oversee kitchen operations as head chef. (Well-liked by the Cochrans' staff, a few years later he became the restaurant manager of the National Press Club in Washington, D.C.) An advertisement published in anticipation of the White Sulphur Springs reopening promised that "the menu at the hotel will be planned with an eye to satisfying the hearty appetite that accompanies outdoor exercise in pure mountain air. The meals will emphasize more than bounty, however. The fine products of Bedford County's farms and markets will be accentuated with the zest of continental flavoring. Many of the vegetables used will be grown in Milligan's

Cove. Jellies, preserves and pastries will be expertly prepared in the Inn's own kitchen."

Initially, the Cochrans attempted to oversee White Sulphur Springs from their homes in Illinois and Ohio, having retained an executive assistant, also formerly with the Drake Hotel, to manage day-to-day operations. A contractors' publication noted that "Cochran, with headquarters in Chicago, will still maintain an active interest in the construction equipment industry." And even several years after the reopening, Paul expressed his intention to return to his previous business "…now that this property is a going concern and it is not at all necessary for its success for me to be here constantly, if at all." However, as he later admitted, "The hotel became much more extensive than planned, ceasing to be a hobby." After experiencing disappointments with incompetent or untrustworthy hired managers, he sold all of his Midwest equipment company interests to be able to devote full attention to White Sulphur Springs. The Cochrans formally moved to Pennsylvania and into the hotel in the early 1960s, in the belief that they should be immediately available in case any of the building's mechanical systems malfunctioned. For the next 15 years, they made their home in a two-room suite at the south end of the second floor. Patricia functioned as the hotel and dining room manager, while Paul saw to the upkeep of the buildings and grounds, and also struggled with a financial picture much different from anything he had encountered in the business of manufacturing road graders and bulldozers.

Throughout the Cochrans' ownership of White Sulphur Springs, area newspapers made much of the fact that romance had been behind their purchase of the resort. It was their devotion to each other and to preserving the history associated with the property which enabled them to bring back to life a facility which many in the area thought would never be revived.

White Sulphur Springs in the Cochran Era

The Cochrans, from the first, sought to recreate the genteel era of traditional small, regional summer resorts and inns, blended with the contemporary sophistication of cosmopolitan society life. Gentlemen were not allowed in the dining room without a jacket at mealtime. Waitresses, drawn from the surrounding area, were carefully instructed by Patricia Cochran in proper table setting and serving techniques. A separate employee dining room was provided adjacent to the kitchen ("chauffeurs served here"). Tea was served regularly in the parlor by Patricia, using her own silver. Lodging guests always found pitchers of spring water on a table in the front lobby, at the foot of the curving stairway leading to the upper floors. At the same time, the Cochrans' approach was considered somewhat more casual than the Colvins' by guests who remembered the resort's earlier days.

For staff, the Cochrans started with a hired manager, an assistant manager, two desk clerks, two night men, four bellmen, a chef and his assistant, two dishwashers, a pantry girl to make desserts and salads, and six waitresses in the dining room, as well as a housekeeper for each upstairs floor. Patricia directed that bedspreads be made from documentary prints, a departure from the plain look maintained by the Colvins. To help preserve the spreads, she insisted on having night service, paying an employee to take the covers off and turn the beds down. This service was particularly appreciated by people traveling alone, she said. The grounds crew consisted of at least three men, with Patricia personally overseeing a cutting garden that produced flowers for the front hall and dining room.

As part of the renovation, the Cochrans installed a new, more efficient heating system. And yet during its first few years of operation, White Sulphur Springs remained a summer-only operation as it had been under Colvin own-

Uniformed bellman, c. 1954.

Announcement

Pennsylvania's White Sulphur Springs Hotel

will remain open the winter of 1954-1955.

Winter rates of twenty percent less than summer rates
will apply for both European and American Plan
(American plan minimum two full days).

Summer Season rates effective April 1st, 1955.

We invite your winter visit.

Mailing Address:
Mann's Choice, Bedford County
Pennsylvania
Telephone: Bedford 848

Hotel kitchen staff; winter opening announcement.

ership, although special groups apparently were accommodated during the winters from 1950 to 1953, served by a skeleton staff. The winter of 1954-55 was the first time that the hotel was advertised as being kept open all winter, with the addition to the inn's recreational offerings of ice skating on the resort's ponds as well as access to nearby skiing. It never closed for the remainder of its years as a public inn.

Of passing interest is a front-page story in the January 26, 1954, *Bedford Gazette* which noted that Paul Cochran had leased several hundred acres in the Milligan's Cove area, apparently for possible oil drilling. The account reported that "...Oil and gas fever again seems to be spreading throughout Bedford County, following the striking of a pocket of gas in the wildcat drilling now going on in the Broad Top area." The term of the lease was said to be for

10 years. Patricia explained later that she and her husband ultimately decided against the project after the first test bore. "They offered to sign an agreement to reimburse us for any damage done," she recalled. "But Paul said our water table and spring were too valuable to disturb."

The Cochrans were faced with the task of rebuilding a business base after the hotel had been closed for nine years. They soon developed an active trade primarily from central Pennsylvania and the Pittsburgh area, counting among their clientele steel industry leaders, lawyers, and other executives and professionals. A few guests from the Colvin years also returned, with one noting in the guest book, "5th generation of family to visit WSS." In addition, while the Colvins had limited their promotion of White Sulphur Springs to brochures and other efforts targeting central Pennsylvania, the Cochrans aggressively advertised their resort throughout the Midwest and East — with lighted billboards along the Turnpike and Lincoln Highway in Pennsylvania, and in Maryland; in travel publications, Pennsylvania and Ohio state magazines, and the newspapers of Pittsburgh, Altoona, and Washington, D.C.; and in the *Hotel and Motel Red Book*. The resort was recommended by AAA and in the widely read Duncan Hines guide, the *Consolidated Tours Hotel Directory*, and *Pennsylvania's Best* magazine, as well as in *Country Inns and Back Roads*.

Advertising slogans devised by the Cochrans effectively summarized their concept of the resort: "Yesterday's atmosphere…today's comforts…tomorrow's memories"; "Atmosphere of Colonial times"; "For Rest and Relaxation in a Sylvan Atmosphere"; "The Place Where Cares Refuse To Stay"; "A Quiet and Restful Haven for the Discriminating Guest"; and, as a gentle admonition to families caught up in the too-busy and still-accelerating pace of life in the

1950s, "Change your vacation habits." Hotel brochures promised that "valet service, room service, chauffeur service and parking service are all available." Employees, including the bell staff, appeared in custom-designed uniforms. Soaps, chocolates, book matches, coasters, sugar cubes, stationery, and other hospitality items all bore a tasteful green "WSS" emblem, as did the dining room china, and guests could choose from more than a dozen postcards of the resort to send to friends back home. Patricia also designed the distinctive shield that graced all outdoor signage after she returned to the inn one day during the late-1940s renovation to discover the hired manager had authorized a version which "looked like a sign from the biggest, cheapest, worst possible saloon you could ever imagine, with all sorts of colors." The trained artist raced upstairs to sketch out what she wanted, and painters soon obliterated the unapproved, offending design, substituting Patricia's creation, which is still used today.

Promotional items and Patricia's sign shield.

Mealtime remained a special event at White Sulphur Springs, living up to the pre-opening billing. Breakfast was served from 7:30 to 9 (a "Rip Van Winkle" breakfast was offered from 9:45 to noon); lunch hours were 12 to 2, and dinner 6 to 8. The individually typed menus prepared by the Cochrans underscored the fact that, as remote as the relatively small resort seemed in its woodland setting, its cuisine was nothing less than might be found at much larger metropolitan hostelries. Breakfasts featured Pennsylvania bacon and country sausage, fresh eggs, stacks of pancakes, and imported coffee. Dinner menu selections often included the house specialty of peanut soup (made according to a recipe from the dining car of the "Orange Blossom Special" New York-to-Miami passenger train), followed by prime rib, Delmonico steak, Smithfield ham, roast Bedford County turkey, vegetables including Blue Lake Green Beans and Harvard Beets, and cakes and pies baked on-site. "And with all pardons to Betty Crocker," Patricia stressed indignantly, "the White Sulphur Springs uses absolutely NO mixes!"

Lunch was generally lighter fare, except on Sunday, when a loyal following of Bedford-area residents made a weekly practice of enjoying a sumptuous mid-day meal at the hotel after church. The Sunday environment was advertised emphatically as "Candlelight Dining (but without canned music!)." Special meals were presented during holidays, with Easter dinner a particularly stylish event. The Cochrans raised their own produce in a two-acre truck garden for the first two years of the hotel's new life but soon found that demand outstripped supply, and efforts to raise their own hogs and maintain a herd of beef cattle were similarly short-lived.

While the Colvins relied on the resort's natural beauty to keep guests occupied, the Cochrans often scheduled dance parties, bringing in professional musicians and other entertainment, although the rural location presented challenges in this regard. On at least one occasion when a group of singers canceled at the last minute, Patricia dressed in a flashy gown and blond wig, and sang a breathy version of "Jenny Would Make Up Her Mind" to surprised, amused guests who included a shocked local clergyman.

The serving of liquor, at first prohibited, seems to have crept into the picture from time to time. In the 1950s, the hotel advertised the limited availability of alcoholic beverages. In deference to those wishing to occasionally lift a libation,

1886
The White Sulphur Springs Hotel
Manns Choice, Bedford County
Pennsylvania

Please observe evening quiet hour beginning 10:30 P. M. Guest stationery and postcards available at the desk. Soft drinks and setups available through the desk. Not served after quiet hour.

Swimming: Beach towels on request at the desk. If guests desire to dress in their rooms it is requested that robes be worn and that while in swimming attire the rear exit be used. There is a beach house at the swimming lake for the purpose of changing clothes.

Smoking: Please be careful.

Announcement . . . .
Pennsylvania's White Sulphur Springs Hotel now is equipped to serve its guests cocktails, wines and other beverages during limited hours.
Also we wish to advise that the fishing pond is well stocked with a good variety for year 'round fishing.

Mailing Address
Mann's Choice-Bedford County
Pennsylvania

Telephone: Bedford 848

Quiet hours reminder and Patricia entertaining guests in the blond wig.

How to Travel With Children

By Orval Hopkins

IT HAS BEEN my theory, resolutely held in the face of accusation and abuse, that the best way to travel with children is to leave the children home. And as I pulled up at the White Sulphur Springs Hotel in Mann's Choice, Pa., the other day I could only reflect that the theory is indeed a durable one, possibly a concept to take its place with another great wheeze of my acquaintance, namely, "Women bother people."

By the time Paul B. Cochran, owner of the White Sulphur Springs, greeted us at the door, we had been scrabbling for eight hours, with four children variously in the rear seat, in the front seat, and just under foot. And I can tell you it took some character.

But arrive we did, and after a shower, a short beer and a fine meal, things were less dim.

The White Sulphur Springs, Cochran told me, was built in 1886. It has been refurbished and kept up to date through the decades and today is a sparkling modern retreat set entirely alone in the Alleghenies only a few miles off the Horseshoe Trail (Route 220). The hotel is the quiet kind (or was until our arrival shattered the primeval peace), which is to say there is no bar. There is, however, no objection to the traveler's importing a spot of grog, as a matter of fact, Cochran is building a sort of lounge-and-bar clubhouse away from the main building. He expects to have it in operation sometime in the fall.

The hotel is bounded on three sides by a broad veranda lined with cozy rockers built from the indigenous woods of the area. In the basement is a spacious recreation room equipped with shuffleboard, pingpong and card tables, the first two of which submitted to a thorough going-over at the tender hands of Sam and Brien (9 and 6). The room also has a huge fireplace and in one corner a piano, which Polly (12) dutifully thumped for 20 minutes one evening.

The plant has a large, irregularly-shaped, spring-fed swimming pool, croquet and horseshoe-pitching grounds, an immaculate clay tennis court and a two-alley bowling building, all of which, with the exception of the tennis court were duly inspected and found more than ample by the children. In fact, I poured down a couple of balls on the bowling alley myself. Scored a strike, naturally. These divertissements were so eminently satisfactory that I generally had to throw one my tantrums in order to tear the children away at mealtime. While there we also inspected a litter of new pigs and a wide pond which Cochran has lately stocked with fish against future seasons.

This spot of grace and beauty can be reached from Washington by proceeding to Hagerstown, taking highway 40 west to Cumberland, then picking up Route 96 north 27 miles, almost to Mann's Choice, and the White Sulphur Springs Hotel sign.

We also had occasion to visit pleasantly with Mrs. Cochran, a woman not only of charm and sincerity but of great courage as well. She offered to wrestle with our other redhead, Daniel Price, now 7 months.

The Washington Post, August 9, 1953

the Cabin Club House became known informally as "The Elbow Room."

Alcohol was never a major resort attraction, although Paul noted that the hotel liquor license differentiated the inn from similar nearby resorts lacking this amenity. The license was eventually dropped because the owners thought it was attracting an undesirable element. Noted one columnist: "This is not a place for a swinger. It is for those who enjoy the quiet, and the peace and beauty of nature." As another reflection of their self-described "old-fashioned" country inn philosophy, the Cochrans maintained guest books rather than formal hotel registers throughout their tenure.

While not brought up or educated in the hotel business, the Cochrans had a natural business sense when it came to hospitality. They were unfailingly gracious hosts who practiced and insisted on courtesy and proper manners. Even today, former employees are quick to express their appreciation for all they learned, while in their teens or 20s, through their association with the Cochrans. Paul kept a file in which he recorded each guest's service preferences so that these could be automatically honored on future visits. A man who held strong opinions and was a keen judge of people, he also noted on the cards any problems caused by guests which could preclude their future accommodation.

Among the Cochrans' favorite visitors was Margaret Landon, who wrote *Anna and The King of Siam*, on which the musical *The King and I* was based, and her husband, as well as U.S. Representative Brooks Hays (Arkansas). Another especially memorable guest was a Crow Indian chief, Ti Kar Nak ("Bent Knife" in the Crow language), who spent summer and autumn days, when he was not roaming the nearby hills and mountains he loved, on the hotel's front porch quietly doing intricate bead-work or sharing with guests his wisdom about life. The son of White Swan, who had been a scout for General Custer in the American Indian Wars, Ti Kar Nak had served in World War I, performing scouting duties for General Pershing. His two sons functioned in the same capacity for General Patton in World War II. Well-known and beloved in the area, Ti Kar Nak devoted many hours to teaching Indian bead-work to the Cumberland, Maryland, school children he dubbed his "little stars."

And then there was Miss Homer who, according to Patricia Cochran, "came for a week or 10 days when the Colvins had White Sulphur Springs…and stayed 20 years." An acquaintance of Michael Colvin's wife Lorena who had worked for the Pennsylvania Railroad and came from a well-to-do family, the overbearing and enigmatic Miss Homer moved to the hotel near the time of Michael Colvin's death and subsequently lived with Lorena in the cottage next door. Disliked by the hotel staff, she was described by one employee as "a sourpuss who never smiled, thought she was better than the others, and always wore a hairnet." Not long after arriving, Miss Homer began presenting herself as the property's manager, both in correspondence and by gruffly issuing orders to the workmen renovating the hotel when the Cochrans were not around. In this unauthorized capacity, she wrote to one company insisting that its ice cream freezer "had rusted immediately," ignoring the fact that, no longer needed, the old appliance had been deliberately left outside all winter. The apologetic company quickly sent a new freezer. Miss Homer's later complaint, again supposedly sent on behalf of White Sulphur Springs and this time dealing with what she considered the shrinking size of toilet tissue rolls, likewise produced a huge crate of the product from the supplier, who at that point undoubtedly was questioning the hotel management's sanity. The Cochrans then discovered she was secretly and inexplicably removing original golden-oak tables from the main building and stashing them in the attic of the cottage. The would-be hotel executive finally relocated to Bedford when Mrs. Colvin, who had grown distrustful of Miss Homer, moved into the main hotel and the Cochrans, with great relief, closed the cottage.

Business meetings and private social functions were actively sought by the Cochrans and were an important income source. Hotel scrapbooks contain dozens of mementos from weddings, antique car shows, high school banquets, and gatherings by Lions and Optimist Clubs, the Rotary, Pennsylvania Society of Architects, professors and students from the University of Pittsburgh and Penn State, and, ironic in view of the resort's feared sale to a log-ger which prompted the Cochrans to buy the property, a workshop for area Lumber Institute executives.

Despite her duties managing the day-to-day operations of the hotel, Patricia Cochran found time to indulge in her favorite pastime of painting; her scenes of the hotel and surrounding countryside still decorate the inn today. She also conducted painting classes several times a week and accepted commissions to paint portraits, with many subjects either posing in person or sending her photographs. One of her largest works, of Christ praying at Gethsemane, adorns the chancel of the Methodist Church in nearby Helixville, Pennsylvania.

Guests from a 1950s antique car rally;
Patricia painting in front of the hotel.

Ti Kar Nak with the author's daughter, 1982; one of his beaded necklaces.

It must be remembered:
The earth is our Mother
From her we come
She will feed us, love us, and make us grow
To her we go home

The Sun is our Father
He will make us big and strong

Our Grandmother is the moon
She is the kind one who
Walks over the sky at night
To carry her light
So that we can see where we go

Our grandfather, he is the great owl
Oh, so wise
If you see in the day
Sleeping in a tree
Always one eye will be open
So he can see what happens in day time also

Family Blood Lines — Ti Kar Nak

Once Again, an Uncertain Future

Over the years, Paul and Patricia Cochran devoted their entire life savings to restoring and operating the White Sulphur Springs Hotel, eventually investing a total of $1 million in this labor of love. Financial struggles were evident early in their ownership of the property, and by 1954, the Cochrans apparently were having serious second thoughts about their new vocation. Letters written by Mr. Cochran suggest he instinctively knew from the first that the venture was unlikely to be a money-maker. In the mid-'50s, a national real estate firm was retained to solicit buyers for "A luxuriously modern resort hotel offered for sale for the first time, completely furnished and equipped — ideal for many uses: hotel, club, health, or recreation center." A sales circular describes newly renovated White Sulphur Springs in detail, attaching a third-party endorsement of the resort's spring water.

Throughout the 1960s and early 1970s, with the couple's financial resources largely drained, Paul Cochran solicited and entertained potential buyers. Many possible uses for the property were discussed. At one point, a racetrack was being considered for the Bedford area, an attraction which could have brought steady additional business, and this proposed project was mentioned by Paul in an effort to interest investors. Other prospects asked about the feasibility of adding golf or a ski lift, and Paul suggested one buyer could economically expand lodging by converting the bowling alley into accommodations for 20 additional guests. At one time or another, parties making inquiry about the property included an Ohio hotel owner, a young Pennsylvania couple with great enthusiasm but no money, a religious order, a "food scientist"/author interested in the powers of mineral waters, a television evangelist, a Pittsburgh meat packer, and a consortium of wealthy Philadelphia businessmen seeking to form a private club. One sharply dressed big-city group of prospects alarmed a staff member by appearing somewhat shady…"like they wanted a place where they could get away and hide."

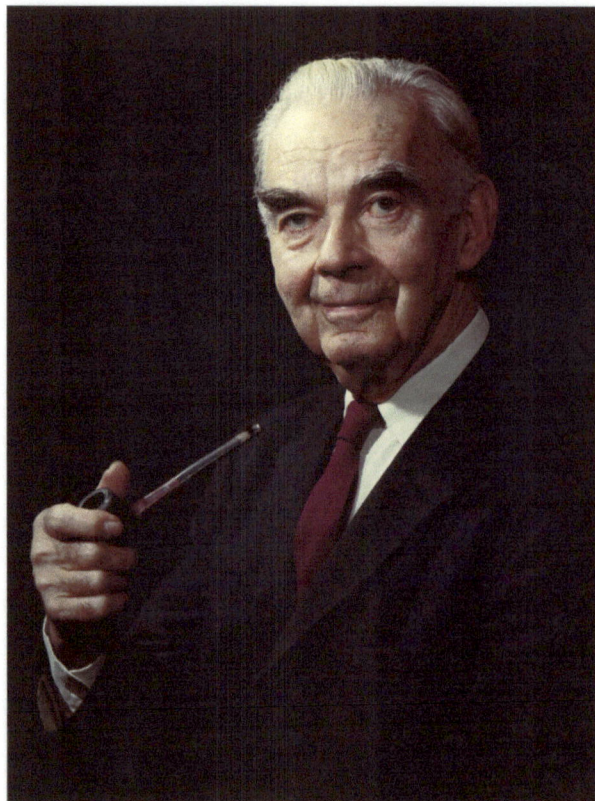

Paul Cochran seemed adamant in his desire to remove himself and his wife from the hotel business. And yet none of the offers or discussions bore fruit; there always seemed to be some element of a proposal which the Cochrans found unacceptable. At the heart of the matter, clearly, was their hope that some means could be found to sustain

The Cochrans in 1967.

White Sulphur Springs in the same form which had fascinated Patricia on her first visit in 1910…and which had led her to encourage her husband to forsake his successful equipment businesses so that they might come to the resort's rescue. "We tried to be so careful," Patricia told a reporter in 1984. "We didn't want anyone to have it who wouldn't love it as much as we have." But their options were running out.

In seeking buyers, the Cochrans readily acknowledged that they had not made the most of the property's business potential and that this was their conscious decision. Paul wrote in a sales offering for the hotel that "golf has not been provided, although a well-known golf architect was retained and laid out a nine hole course." Their concern for the environment outweighed financial gain.

"Since 1950," Paul wrote in 1969 to a would-be purchaser, "we have been operating as a quiet, reserved country inn. We have never operated as a hotel, that is to take in all and any guests that wished to come here." It was an approach that helped preserve White Sulphur Springs but limited the bottom line. In a 1971 letter to the president of a Piqua, Ohio, felt company who had inquired about the property, Paul Cochran elaborated upon the philosophy which had guided the couple's management style for two decades. "For instance, we will not take the ski groups that roar in on weekends and make a shambles of where ever they go. The same applies to the many others who think this is a perfect spot, remote, yet accessible, for 'shacking up' for a few days. To get rid of some of this element is why we dropped our liquor license several years ago. Hence from a financial standpoint, there never has been any 'profit.' We have made our depreciation figure, but never a profit as we think of it in business." Their motivation for purchasing the original property, he stressed, was "to preserve."

As the hotel approached its centennial, changing travel trends had placed severe stress on small, independently owned inns in general. Stays at White Sulphur Springs were of shorter duration, with fewer guests traveling long distances than in years past although the hotel limousine still occasionally met planes at Altoona and Johnstown.

Once Again, an Uncertain Future • 73

In addition, health problems were making it increasingly difficult for Paul and Patricia, both well past 65, to operate a facility which, although they had modernized it many years before, was again beginning to show its age. By the early 1970s, only the White Sulphur Springs dining room remained in full operation, still enjoying a brisk Sunday dinner trade. Daily room rates had increased to $16-$24 for singles and $27.50 to $45 for doubles, all including three meals, but fewer overnight guests were accommodated, and such business was no longer actively solicited. Norman Simpson, author of *Country Inns and Back Roads*, sadly noted in a mid-'70s letter to other acquaintances of the Cochrans, "While I am very much attached to the people that run it, at the same time I am keenly aware of the shortcomings that the inn has."

And yet the Cochrans were encouraged by visits of old friends, who were often the only occupants of the guest rooms and continued to be charmed by what had become, in essence, a "bed and breakfast." On blustery winter nights, Paul Cochran, a bushy-eyebrowed man with a seemingly gruff exterior but a kind and generous disposition, could be found seated with his wife before a roaring fire in the Big Room, smoking his ever-present pipe and beguiling guests with colorful tales of his younger

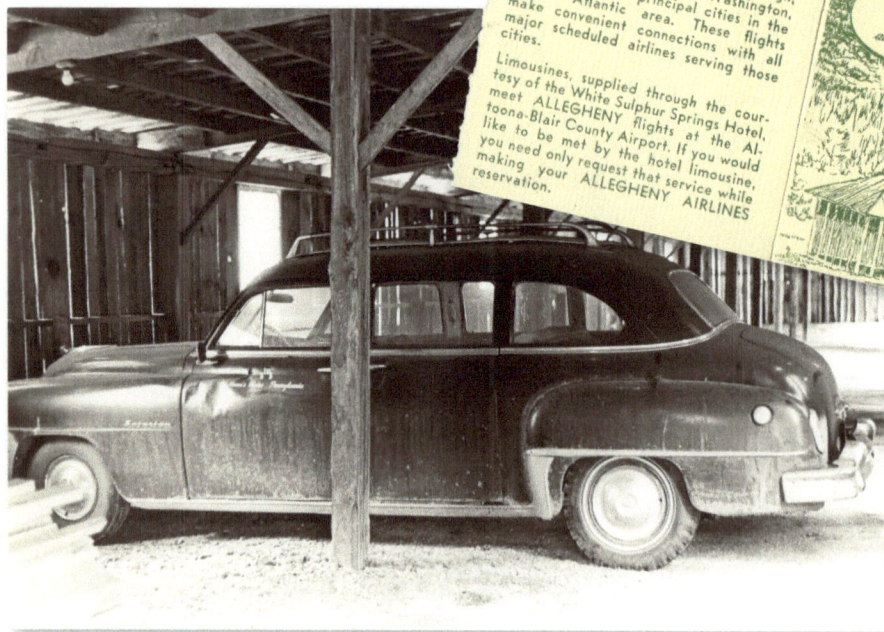

You're just an easy flight from delightful White Sulphur Springs.

ALLEGHENY AIRLINES offers convenient scheduled service from Pittsburgh, New York, Philadelphia, Washington, D. C., and other principal cities in the Middle Atlantic area. These flights make convenient connections with all major scheduled airlines serving those cities.

Limousines, supplied through the courtesy of the White Sulphur Springs Hotel, meet ALLEGHENY flights at the Altoona-Blair County Airport. If you would like to be met by the hotel limousine, you need only request that service while making your ALLEGHENY AIRLINES reservation.

1886
The White Sulphur
Springs Hotel
at Milligans Cove, Pa.

TYPICAL AIR TRAVEL TIME* SELECTED CITIES TO ALTOONA-BLAIR COUNTY AIRPORT	
BALTIMORE, MD.	2 Hrs. 40 Min.
BOSTON, MASS.	5 Hrs. 20 Min.
BUFFALO, N. Y.	3 Hrs. 17 Min.
CHICAGO, ILL.	4 Hrs. 17 Min.
CINCINNATI, OHIO	3 Hrs. 55 Min.
COLUMBUS, OHIO	3 Hrs. 29 Min.
DAYTON, OHIO	3 Hrs. 9 Min.
DETROIT, MICH.	2 Hrs. 41 Min.
INDIANAPOLIS, IND.	4 Hrs. 10 Min.
NEW YORK, N. Y.	2 Hrs. 22 Min.
PHILADELPHIA, PA.	1 Hr. 32 Min.
PITTSBURGH, PA.	57 Min.
ST. LOUIS, MO.	4 Hrs. 47 Min.
WASHINGTON, D. C.	1 Hr. 39 Min.

*includes standard 30 minute connections.

Fly ALLEGHENY, and add a day or two to your visit in delightful White Sulphur Springs.

An Allegheny Airlines cross-promotion; the hotel limousine, a 1951 DeSoto Suburban, showing its age in 1974; Right: a hotel postcard from the Cochran era.

days, of Chicago at its industrial peak, and of the couple's experiences at White Sulphur Springs. Patricia Cochran sometimes joined in but generally was content to let her husband hold the floor.

Finally, Paul's failing health prompted his doctors to firmly advise the couple to give up the intensive burden of management and move south. The Cochrans found themselves encountering what Lorena Colvin had experienced more than 30 years earlier after the death of her husband Michael: With no children or other family members to follow in their footsteps, they faced the prospect of being forced to sell White Sulphur Springs to outsiders, probably to waiting lumber companies eager to harvest the hundreds of acres of prime timber. They and anxious friends sought but initially failed to find a suitable buyer. The Cochrans prayed, especially for a Christian group which would appreciate the heritage of White Sulphur Springs and preserve the Lord's work — the beauty and serenity which had attracted guests for generations.

Meanwhile, Officers' Christian Fellowship (OCF), which had operated a Colorado conference center since the 1960s, had made the decision several years earlier to seek a comparable location in the eastern United States to support and expand its ministry. OCF's search began along the Chesapeake Bay, moved to the Blue Ridge Mountains, and finally focused in the fall of 1977 on a newly discovered possibility near Bedford, Pennsylvania. Former OCF president Rear Admiral Robert L. Baughan, Jr., U.S. Navy, was retired and living in the central part of the state, working for the Central

Pennsylvania Synod of the Lutheran Church of America and visiting churches in the area. While driving near Bedford one day, he recalled a conversation with a Synod representative who mentioned she heard that the Cochrans might be interested in selling their resort. Knowing OCF was having difficulty finding a suitable place, he dropped by White Sulphur Springs and met its owners. More visits by OCF members followed; OCF made an offer; and the Cochrans, impressed by the prospective purchasers' faith and commitment, finally accepted. They later told an acquaintance that they made their decision after Paul was hospitalized in Washington, D.C. and OCF members spent hours there praying with them, even though no agreement regarding White Sulphur Springs was certain.

"You know, these people are real," Paul remarked admiringly. "They don't put their religion on just on Sundays. They're very genuine. I think we'd better decide on them."

Winter at
The White Sulphur Springs Hotel

OFFICERS' CHRISTIAN FELLOWSHIP ASSUMES COMMAND

Events moved swiftly, once the Cochrans reached an agreement with OCF, and the transfer officially occurred on March 17, 1978. Formal dedication services signifying the ownership change were held on June 18, 1978, with the Cochrans joining OCF representatives in addressing 200 invited guests. Steps were soon taken to update the various systems in the main building and otherwise prepare the entire facility for its new role as a meeting and retreat center for OCF members, and the first ministry programs were conducted shortly thereafter. Knowing that White Sulphur Springs would remain in good hands, Paul Cochran joined the Lord in peace later that year.

Throughout her life, Patricia Cochran carried herself with the dignity and refinement that led one admiring interviewer to describe the Pennsylvania native as "a distinguished looking English lady." Following Paul's death, she assumed from him the role of story-teller, delighting in sharing with visitors her recollections of White Sulphur Springs, including accounts of how she and her husband brought the dormant resort back to life.

Many years earlier, the Cochrans had set aside 10 acres of land near the hotel, intending to build a stone colonial retirement house in the pines. Patricia chose not to pursue that course by herself, and not wishing to return to a large metropolitan area, she sought unsuccessfully to find a house in Bedford. OCF then offered her the option of living permanently in the cottage next door to the main hotel, and she readily accepted. She subsequently renovated the cottage, extending the living room and adding a master bedroom as well as an art studio.

As Major General Clay T. Buckingham, U.S. Army, Retired, a former OCF president and an early White Sulphur Springs center director, recounted in remarks to the organization's Council, the OCF staff immediately em-

The Cochrans with Major General Buckingham, 1978.

braced Patricia as one of their ministry family, and she, having no natural offspring of her own or other living relatives (although she had countless godchildren), adopted the staff as her children. From 1978 until her death in May 1995, "Miss Pat," as she was affectionately known, was fully a part of the White Sulphur Springs ministry, providing an important link to the earliest days of the hotel. She regularly took part in OCF programs and frequently entertained OCF staff and guests during elegant "Strawberry Teas" in her parlor. Particularly during her favorite season of spring, Patricia could be found chatting with friends on the front porch of the cottage, where Lorena Colvin also had spent many happy hours years before.

Following Patricia's passing, the cottage was converted to several new uses. Her beautifully furnished formal living room was retained for Bible study groups and other OCF meetings, while the bedroom provided lodging for visiting speakers and program leaders. Her artist's studio, of which she was so proud, became the White Sulphur Springs museum and archives, its walls filled with her paintings and its display cases, made of cherry wood from trees grown on the property, containing artifacts from the inn's long history.

Elsewhere at White Sulphur Springs, the former hotel building was designated "Harrison House" by OCF in honor of Lieutenant General William K. Harrison, Jr., U.S. Army, Retired, and his wife Eva. The Harrisons had served for 18 years as president and first lady of OCF. The two-story log house constructed in the 1950s was named "Fort Cochran" to recognize the previous owners and was dedicated to the service and glory of Lord Jesus Christ. The spring would later be named in honor of the Colvin family.

OCF, in assuming ownership of the former resort, discovered many of the same challenges that faced the Cochrans in the late 1940s — specifically, a physical plant in need of substantial updating, although it was understood that any changes had to be in keeping with the ambiance which is one of the property's greatest assets. Fire and emergency systems were upgraded; out-buildings, some of which had not been used for years, were reactivated or converted to fulfill new functions; and mechanical systems in Harrison House were replaced.

Because of its location, White Sulphur Springs rapidly became a key center of OCF ministry for the Washington, D.C. area and the East Coast military service academies. Members and their families could escape the Beltway lifestyle via a scenic three-hour drive to a weekend or week of rest and Christian fellowship in the Pennsylvania moun-

Officers' Christian Fellowship of the U.S.A. (OCF), which has owned and operated White Sulphur Springs as its eastern conference center since 1978, was founded during World War II as Officers' Christian Union, with the objectives of binding together Christian officers; helping all ranks, grades, and ratings to come to a knowledge of Jesus Christ; and stimulating prayer, Bible study, and Christian witness.

Today, OCF has over 15,000 members. OCF groups meet at military installations around the world to encourage and equip members for effective ministry to the entire military society. OCF maintains conference centers at White Sulphur Springs and at Spring Canyon in Colorado, and leaders within OCF groups often have been trained at these centers. The OCF home office is located in Englewood, Colorado.

tains. Personnel from other military installations throughout the eastern United States soon became acquainted with the warmth and hospitality of the center and its staff, and an extensive summer camping program was instituted. Continuing the practice begun by the Cochrans, OCF operates White Sulphur Springs on a year-round basis.

By the early 1990s, the White Sulphur Springs conference center was providing 10 weeks of summer seminars for families and individuals; multiple sessions of "Allegheny Outback" teen adventure camps; three weeks of family winter retreat; an Easter retreat; a retirement ministries conference; a home schoolers' seminar; and numerous academy and ROTC cadet and midshipmen retreats. OCF and chapel groups in the eastern region regularly visited White Sulphur Springs for weekend retreats, as did a number of area church groups. Twice a year, in spring and fall, OCF volunteers came to the center to renovate existing facilities, build new ones, and enjoy fellowship as they worked.

In 1993, following a successful fund drive, OCF purchased a 500-acre parcel adjoining the original conference center land. This acquisition expanded the property to 1,050 acres and provided vast potential for additional program activities.

In succeeding years, OCF's ministry at White Sulphur Springs has steadily grown. Guests now include the children, and in some cases grandchildren, of the generation of OCF members who were led to make the venerable hotel property a key component of the organization's ministry in the 1970s. OCF has established strong ties with the Bedford community, and the White Sulphur Springs Fourth of July picnic and Christmas Open House attract

hundreds of area residents, a number of whom worked at or were guests in the hotel in years past.

Today, the broad porch with its comfy rockers still serves as a restful spot for reflection and prayer. The dining room bustles at mealtime and for evening snacks, with guests enjoying food prepared, as in decades past, by skilled cooks from the Milligan's Cove and Mann's Choice area. Laughter and the crash of pins can be heard across the road in the bowling alley. And from deep in the surrounding forest, calls from unseen wildlife remind all of the obligation, fulfilled so well by so many for so long, to sustain and nurture this remarkable piece of Americana, for the glory of God and for the benefit of this and future generations.

Scenes from OCF activities at White Sulphur Springs.

A Look Ahead for White Sulphur Springs

Well into its second century, White Sulphur Springs has both a distinguished past and a promising future. Stewarded first by the Colvin family, then by Paul and Patricia Cochran, and now by Officers' Christian Fellowship, the building now known as Harrison House welcomes a larger number of guests each summer than during its busiest years as a public hotel, with demand often exceeding capacity. Given the growth of its ministry, OCF has embarked on an ambitious fundraising program to construct a new, larger "Heritage House" lodge, both to accommodate more guests and to relieve summer group pressure borne by the original building. The new lodge's site is not far from the location of the old log hotel where the hospitality business got its start in Milligan's Cove in the 1700s, and its design captures the feel of a nineteenth century resort. OCF's "Growing and Building" campaign also will provide funds to expand facilities at its Spring Canyon, Colorado, conference center, and it will create an endowment for scholarships to help cadets, midshipmen, and young military families attend programs at the centers.

Even as plans proceed for the new Heritage House, longtime visitors to White Sulphur Springs during the Colvin, Cochran, and OCF eras are encouraged to know that the future of Harrison House is secure. Through an endowment established by friends of OCF and White Sulphur Springs to support ongoing operational costs, the 1880s landmark, including all the original out-buildings, will be carefully maintained in a reduced-use status, serving OCF ministry needs in various ways, including the accommodation of smaller meeting groups and perhaps an expanded museum. As such, Harrison House will remain the "historic heart" of White Sulphur Springs so that OCF members and friends of the hotel can be reminded of the godly spirit and commitment of men and women, from years gone by and continuing today, to seeing that the legendary inn and its lushly wooded grounds remain, as OCF describes it, "A Place Apart, A Place Of The Heart."

The spring house and hotel, early 1900s and 2009.

ACKNOWLEDGMENTS

Where Cares Refuse To Stay: The Story of Pennsylvania's White Sulphur Springs Hotel owes its existence, first and foremost, to generations of caring, committed people for whom the concepts of "hospitality" and "service" are much more than mere words. They have built sturdy structures which have withstood severe Pennsylvania winters. They have created the welcoming atmosphere which first attracted people to Milligan's Cove centuries ago and continues to do so today. And they have demonstrated the meaning of true "living history" by preserving and honoring the past while carefully making adaptations so that nineteenth-century buildings can continue to perform useful functions in the twenty-first century.

The author is deeply indebted to many people for the contents of this book. Among them:

• Officers' Christian Fellowship (OCF), which today operates White Sulphur Springs as its eastern conference center, has been wonderfully supportive of this book and the White Sulphur Springs Museum and Archives. Long-time Conference Center Executive Director Clay Thomas, Commander, U.S. Navy, Retired, and his wife Marty, together with their outstanding staff, have made innumerable contributions, ranging from tracking down original hotel registers to identifying locations in vintage photographs. Their close friendship is an ongoing blessing.

• Mark F. Heiman, co-owner of Loomis House Press, Northfield, Minnesota, handled the graphic design, illustration selection, and printing of this book with typical patience and creativity, gently keeping us on track in terms of content and format. Like his wife Laura (the author's daughter and a frequent visitor to Milligan's Cove through the years), Mark has come to know and appreciate the special place that is White Sulphur Springs and the special people who have nurtured and preserved it. The book's appearance testifies to his remarkable skill in photography, photo restoration, scanning, layout, and overall project coordination. We are lucky to have him in our family.

• An out-of-the-blue e-mail sent to John M. Colvin, grandson of White Sulphur Springs Hotel co-owner R. Ross Colvin, sparked the exchange of hundreds of communications as this book progressed, creating a lasting friendship between John, the Saxton and Heiman families, and OCF. Together, we have explored Colvin involvement in the resort's first years, along the way discovering common interests that produced such esoteric details as the year, make, and model of the White Sulphur Springs DeSoto limousine. John has graciously shared century-old photos as well as family facts and anecdotes which have allowed more in-depth characterization of the early owners. He has also been an astute proofreader. We are grateful he is a partner in this ongoing initiative to tell the story of his grandfather's hotel.

• The late Paul and Patricia Cochran, who owned the White Sulphur Springs Hotel from 1946 to 1978, helped prepare the foundation for this book by carefully retaining documents associated with White Sulphur Springs dating back to its opening in the late 1880s, as well as land deeds and other items from much earlier years. Their scrapbooks and files provided invaluable source material. (More of the Cochrans' first-person accounts of their experiences at White Sulphur Springs may be found in the book *Two Lives of Devotion*, available from the bookstore of Officers' Christian Fellowship, White Sulphur Springs, 4499 Milligan's Cove Road, Mann's Choice, Pennsylvania 15550.)

• Lieutenant General Bruce L. Fister, U.S. Air Force, Retired, the executive director of Officers' Christian Fellowship, graciously agreed to provide the foreword to this book and has unceasingly demonstrated a keen interest in history while leading OCF in implementing God's will in the work undertaken at White Sulphur Springs and throughout the ministry.

• Major General Clay T. Buckingham, U.S. Army, Retired, who resides in one of the historic homes of Milligan's Cove and was one of the first OCF White Sulphur Springs center directors, shared his wonderful maps and knowledge of the area, also conducting us on a walking tour of the Abraham May Mountain House site. "General B." and his wife Clara personify Milligan's Cove hospitality.

• A visit to the Web site bbandbrr.com put us in touch with Webmaster Keith Burkey, whose encyclopedic knowledge of Bedford-area railroads, particularly the Huntingdon & Broad Top Mountain, helped pin down many dates associated with the early years of White Sulphur Springs and rail transportation to the resort.

• Valuable information about the May family of Milligan's Cove was provided by Lucy Turner Cronin, who maintains the excellent Web site bedfordconnection.org; and Bonnie Cornell. Lucy and Bonnie both are great-great granddaughters of Hezekiah May, owner of the Arlington Cottage Hotel, a predecessor of the White Sulphur Springs Hotel; great-great-great granddaughters of Daniel May, Jr., who also operated an early hotel in Milligan's Cove; and distant cousins of Charlotte Reed, whose brother John P. Reed was responsible, with the Lyon family, for construction of the White Sulphur Springs Hotel.

• Judge Carson Brown, the great-great grandson of Hezekiah May, took time from his busy schedule to visit White Sulphur Springs, share mementos of Mr. May, and help us unravel the early history of the May boarding houses in Milligan's Cove.

• The Bedford County (Pennsylvania) Historical Society and its excellent researcher Dr. Ray Jackson patiently, cheerfully, and meticulously responded to many requests for information about Bedford and residents of the area, as well as news accounts of White Sulphur Springs, many from 100 or more years ago.

• Helen Waugerman Foor, who had the unique experience of working for both Michael and Lorena Colvin and, years later, Paul and Patricia Cochran, willingly shared her memories of White Sulphur Springs from two key periods in its history. A warm and engaging lady, she has helped bring to life the descriptions of the atmosphere and people of White Sulphur Springs in the early 1940s and in the 1960s–70s.

• Several other former White Sulphur Springs Hotel employees and area residents were also kind enough to share their experiences, including Virginia Leydig Lankey, Carl May, Chester Hillegass, Robert Felton, Larry Burkett, and Jim Hyde.

• Ned Frear, retired publisher of the venerable *Bedford Gazette*, generously allowed us to draw from his excellent series of books outlining the fascinating history of Bedford and environs.

• Barbara Pensyl, Food Services Manager at White Sulphur Springs, and her son Jock gave us access to their unparalleled collection of White Sulphur Springs Hotel postcards.

• The Office of the Bedford County Register and Recorder efficiently accessed and forwarded deeds which helped determine the sequence of White Sulphur Springs land transactions.

• For their diligence in reviewing text and providing insightful comments, we are most appreciative to Cora Allen; OCF Director of Communications Michael Edwards; Dr. Jacqueline Erwin; Wayne King; and Gail Saxton.

• We drew from the written works of the late Roy Kegg, Mann's Choice-area historian, whose carefully recorded facts and anecdotes offer a glimpse into the region's colorful early days.

• John C. Egolf, great-great grandson of Abraham May (owner of the Mountain House) and great-grandson of Watson Diehl (master builder of the White Sulphur Springs hotel), provided firsthand impressions of the abandoned Mountain House, which he had explored as a child.

• Joy and Maurice Fisher, whose home for many years was the former Hezekiah May Arlington Cottage Hotel, shared photos and information about the historic structure, now owned by OCF.

• We salute the residents of Milligan's Cove, Mann's Choice, and environs, whose newly formed Milligan's Cove Historical Society is actively engaged in chronicling the fascinating story of the area. Mary Annette Palmer-Garland, a Society member, was extremely helpful in providing leads for information about the early cove boarding houses. Through Annette, we met Dolores Wisegarver Holler, a former Mann's Choice resident who shared important illustrations, including a drawn portrait of her great-grandparents, Abraham and Sarah May.

• We also honor the memory of the late Norman Simpson, whose *Country Inns and Back Roads* directory first led this author and his family down the winding road to White Sulphur Springs in 1971.

Do you have information, photographs, or other artifacts pertaining to Pennsylvania's White Sulphur Springs Hotel or the earlier Milligan's Cove boarding houses? We would love to hear from you. Please contact us at

wss@loomishousepress.com

ILLUSTRATION CREDITS

Where no credit is indicated, illustrations were obtained from the White Sulphur Springs Museum & Archives or the author's collection.

Bedford County Historical Society: 21, 28 (advertisement)

Carson V. Brown: 19 (Arlington Cottage Hotel card), 39 (railroad excursion ticket)

Keith Burkey: 37 (the original Sulphur Springs station)

John M. Colvin: 24, 25, 30, 33, 38 (tennis players and other guests), 39 (photo), 42, 81 (early 1900s spring house photo)

Mark F. Heiman: Front cover, 11, 36 (bowling alley interior), 81 (2009 spring house photo), 91

Dolores Wisegarver Holler: 20 (Abraham and Sarah May)

Larry G. McKee: Back cover (barn scene)

Officers' Christian Fellowship: 78, 79

Barbara and Jock Pensyl: 13, 14, 15, 17, 18 (Kinton's Knob postcard), 20 (Hezekiah's Backbone postcard), 35 (hotel postcard), 40 (postcard), 43 (postcard), 44 (The Pines postcard), 54, 75

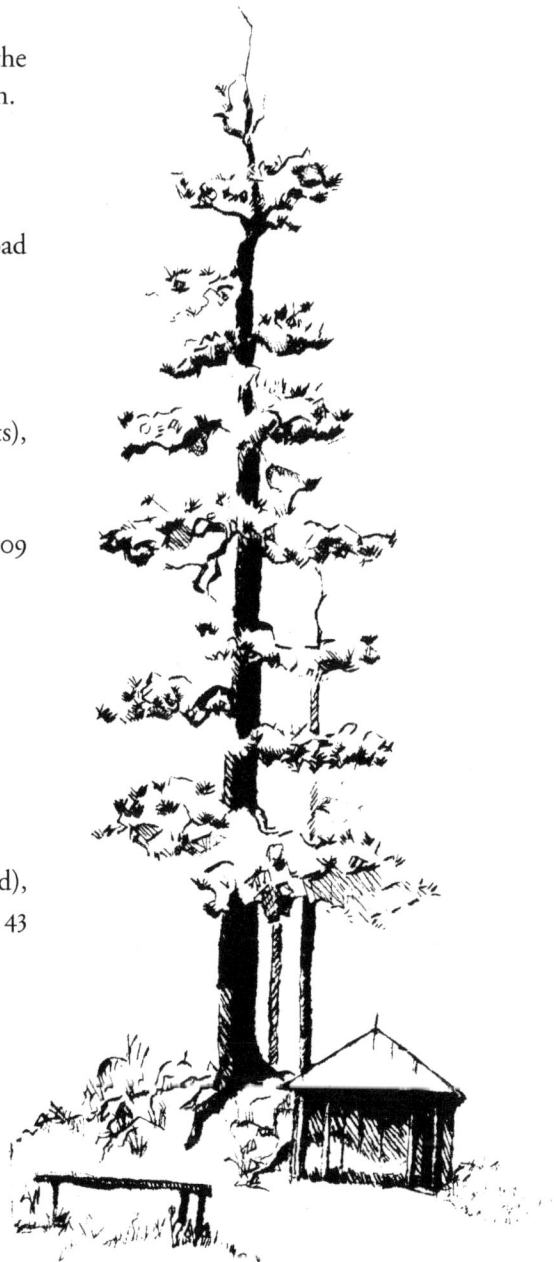

Drawing of "Big Mike" by Patricia Cochran.

White Sulphur Springs Hotel and Predecessors — A Timeline

c. 1770 A log hotel is built along the Packers' Path, a quarter-mile from current White Sulphur Springs hotel site, considered the beginning of the hospitality industry in Milligan's Cove.

1847 William Lyon and Samuel M. Barclay acquire land in Milligan's Cove on which a sulphur spring, one of several in the area, is located. Tract consists of approximately 50 acres.

mid-1800s Daniel May, Jr. opens log boarding house in Milligan's Cove.

1871 William Lyon and John P. Reed become co-owners of the Reed & Lyon White Sulphur Spring, on the tract which Lyon and Samuel M. Barclay acquired in 1847. The property at this point has no buildings.

1872 Abraham M. May builds "Mountain House" for summer boarders.

1874 Hezekiah E. May's "Arlington Cottage Hotel" boarding house opens.

1884–86 John P. Reed and Catharine Lyon, William Lyon's widow, initiate construction of White Sulphur Springs Hotel building.

1887 June 17: Two-story White Sulphur Springs Hotel officially opens for business; Charlotte May, sister of John P. Reed, is manager.

1888 May: Michael and Ross Colvin, nephews of John P. Reed, enter into agreement to manage White Sulphur Springs Hotel. They do so with the help of their sisters, Annie, Ella, Emma, Nina, and Phebe Colvin.

1893–94 Fall–Spring: Third story is added to White Sulphur Springs Hotel building; center wing is added, providing indoor sanitary facilities as well as hot and cold sulphur baths; second- and third-floor rooms are added over expanded kitchen area.

1894 June: Michael and Ross Colvin, together with sisters Annie, Phebe, Nina, and Ella, purchase Sulphur Springs Hotel Property tract from John P. Reed and George M. Lyon, son of Catharine Lyon.

1901 March: Colvins purchase Peter Wertz Sulphur Springs tract of slightly over 50 acres adjoining the Hotel Property tract.

1910 June 14–July 16: Patricia Patterson (later Patricia Cochran), age 5, visits White Sulphur Springs for the first time with her mother.

1911 October 25: Michael Colvin marries Lorena Smelker. November 24: Ross Colvin marries Virginia Hurley.

1913 June: Ross Colvin sells his White Sulphur Springs interests to his sisters Annie, Phebe, and Ella, and relocates with his wife to a farm near Brooks Mills, Pennsylvania.

1928 June: Michael Colvin purchases 40 adjoining acres from B.F. Madore and Jo. W. Tate.

1937 April 24: Pennsylvania Railroad passenger service to Sulphur Springs station is discontinued.

1940 April 13: Ella, last of the five Colvin sisters, dies.

1941 November 2: Final guest registers at Colvin's White Sulphur Springs Hotel; 1942 season still anticipated.

1942 April 18: Michael Colvin dies; his widow Lorena decides not to open the hotel for 1942 season.

1946 September: Paul Cochran purchases White Sulphur Springs Hotel buildings and 140 acres from Lorena Colvin.

1950 July 1: Restored White Sulphur Springs Hotel opens for business.

1950–63 Paul Cochran expands White Sulphur Springs land holdings to 630 acres through a series of purchases of adjoining tracts.

1954–55 White Sulphur Springs Hotel remains open all winter for the first time; previously, it was open from late spring to early fall.

1955 Cochrans open Cabin Club House behind the main hotel building constructed in the style of a Pennsylvania log cabin; used for meetings and recreational activities.

1978 March 17: Stewardship of White Sulphur Springs is transferred from Paul and Patricia Cochran to Officers' Christian Fellowship. June 18: Formal dedication services are held, with the first OCF seminars conducted at White Sulphur Springs that summer.

1978 November 19: Paul Cochran dies; Patricia continues to reside in cottage next door to hotel.

1993 October: OCF expands its White Sulphur Springs Conference Center through the acquisition of 500 adjoining acres; OCF property now encompasses a total of 1,050 acres.

1995 May 19: Patricia Cochran dies.

2009 OCF proceeds with plans for new Heritage House main lodge while preserving and maintaining all of the original White Sulphur Springs facilities, including the former hotel building now known as "Harrison House."

Nov. 1955 newspaper ad.

A GENEALOGY OF THE
COLVIN, REED, AND
MAY FAMILIES

George Colvin ———— Elizabeth McDowell
1775–1848   1788–1861

Jane Colvin
1805–1852

James Colvin
1809–1831

Charlotte Colvin
1807–1870

Eliza Colvin
1811–1874

William H. Colvin
1812–1898

George M. Colvin
1816–1892

Charles W. Colvin
1819–1897

Margaret Colvin
?–?

Reuben Ross Colvin ————
1824–1899

John Edwin Colvin
1830–1892

Michael Reed ———— Elizabeth Sch
1788–1872   1794–1854

Elizabeth Reed
1815–1896

John Philip Reed
1817–1908

Maria Catharine Reed
1819–1900

Jacob Reed
1821–1905

Joseph Schell Reed
1823–1912

Abraham Michael Reed
1826–1853

Margaret S. Reed
1828–1908

Charlotta Reed————
1830–1908

Elinore Reed
1833–?

Peter Andrew Reed
1835–?

George B. Colvin
1849

Emma Virginia Colvin
1850–1935

Eliza Anna Colvin
1852–1920

John Edwin Colvin
1855–1857

Phebe Caroline Colvin
1857–1927

Reuben Ross Colvin ———— Mary Virginia Hurley
1859–1923   1882–1980

Nina Charlotte Colvin
1862–1896

Ella Margaret Colvin
1864–1940

Jacob Reed Colvin
1867–1888

Michael Schell Colvin
1869–1942

Patricia (Patterson) Cochran and Lorena
(Smelker) Colvin are believed to be cousins, but
the exact relationship is not known.

Patricia Lucille Patterson ·························· Lorena Marie Smelker ———— Michael Schell Colvin
1904–1995   1878–1961   1869–1942

male Colvin
15 NOV 1913

Michael Schell Colvin, Jr.
1915–1919

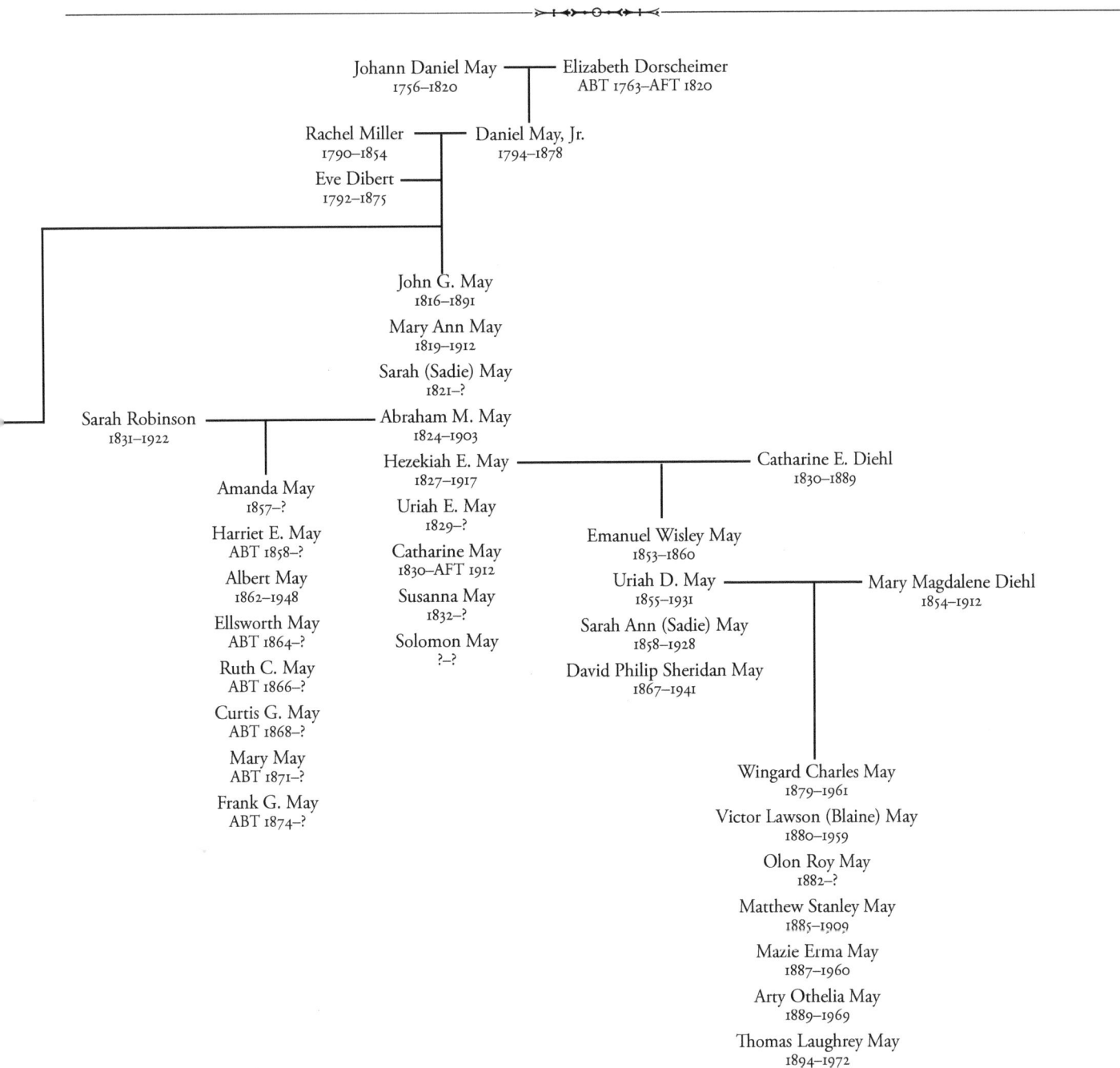

Johann Daniel May ——— Elizabeth Dorscheimer
1756–1820   ABT 1763–AFT 1820

Rachel Miller ——— Daniel May, Jr.
1790–1854   1794–1878
Eve Dibert ———
1792–1875

John G. May
1816–1891

Mary Ann May
1819–1912

Sarah (Sadie) May
1821–?

Sarah Robinson ——— Abraham M. May
1831–1922   1824–1903

Hezekiah E. May ——————————— Catharine E. Diehl
1827–1917   1830–1889

Amanda May
1857–?

Harriet E. May   Uriah E. May
ABT 1858–?   1829–?

Albert May   Catharine May   Emanuel Wisley May
1862–1948   1830–AFT 1912   1853–1860

Ellsworth May   Susanna May   Uriah D. May ——— Mary Magdalene Diehl
ABT 1864–?   1832–?   1855–1931   1854–1912

Ruth C. May   Solomon May   Sarah Ann (Sadie) May
ABT 1866–?   ?–?   1858–1928

Curtis G. May   David Philip Sheridan May
ABT 1868–?   1867–1941

Mary May
ABT 1871–?

Frank G. May
ABT 1874–?

Wingard Charles May
1879–1961

Victor Lawson (Blaine) May
1880–1959

Olon Roy May
1882–?

Matthew Stanley May
1885–1909

Mazie Erma May
1887–1960

Arty Othelia May
1889–1969

Thomas Laughrey May
1894–1972

WHITE SULPHUR SPRINGS — A WALKING TOUR

1. The spring pavilion protects the historic mineral spring (originally the Reed & Lyon White Sulphur Spring) which was known to Shawnee Indians and early Milligan's Cove settlers well before the White Sulphur Springs Hotel was built. For many years, residents of the Cove and surrounding areas regularly visited the spring to refill bottles with the famous water. In honor of White Sulphur Springs' longtime owners, it now carries the name "Colvin's White Sulphur Spring."

2. Harrison House, the main White Sulphur Springs Hotel building, opened for business as a two-story structure in 1887; the third story was added in 1893-94. Today, the hotel continues to provide lodging accommodations, a dining room, a book shop, and recreational/meeting facilities for Officers' Christian Fellowship (OCF), retaining its Colonial atmosphere. It is named in honor of Lieutenant General William K. Harrison, Jr., U.S. Army, Retired, former OCF president, and his wife Eva.

3. The cottage next door to Harrison House was constructed at approximately the same time as the two-story main hotel building. It boasts three side-by-side front doors, with the center door leading to the second floor, apparently to allow use of the three upper-level bedrooms and sleeping porch for overflow hotel guests. The cottage originally served as a hotel office and later housed members of the Colvin family, the proprietors of White Sulphur Springs. Paul and Patricia Cochran purchased the resort from Lorena Colvin in 1946 and sold it to Officers' Christian Fellowship in 1978. After Paul Cochran's death, the cottage continued as the residence of his widow Patricia, a beloved member of the OCF family. Following her death in 1995, the building was converted to serve OCF ministry needs. Mrs. Cochran's art studio now houses the White Sulphur Springs Museum and Archives (open by appointment). A guest bedroom is utilized for program speakers, while the parlor is used for Bible study groups and other small meetings. One side of the first floor is now a children's classroom, while staff housing occupies the second floor. The built-in basement is used as a dormitory for male staff members.

4. The small building next to the cottage was originally the resort's smokehouse, with hams smoked by a fire below. Today, it houses a youth classroom.

5. The former cold storage building with its foot-thick, cork-lined walls, built by the Cochrans and fitted by a Chicago firm with equipment for handling and curing meat, poultry, and other food products, now functions as a workshop for OCF maintenance projects.

6. Fort Cochran, the Pennsylvania log-cabin design style located behind Harrison House, was built by the Cochrans in the early 1950s and is used for Bible study, meetings, square dances, and other ministry activities. It is named for Paul and Patricia Cochran, who owned White Sulphur Springs from 1946 until Officers' Christian Fellowship acquired it in 1978.

7. The long garage building along the service road between the cottage and Fort Cochran houses OCF vehicles and maintenance equipment. When White Sulphur Springs was a public hotel, it also sheltered horse-drawn carriages (termed "real station wagons" by Patricia Cochran) and later a black 1951 9-passenger DeSoto Suburban limousine emblazoned with the White Sulphur Springs crest. Through the years, the hotel conveyances transported guests to and from the railroad stations at Sulphur Springs, Mann's Choice, Bedford, Altoona, and Pittsburgh, Pennsylvania, as well as Cumberland, Maryland; the Pittsburgh, Altoona, Johnstown, and Harrisburg airports; and the Cumberland and Bedford bus stations.

8. Beyond the garage is the White Sulphur Springs fishing lake, also used for ice skating in winter.

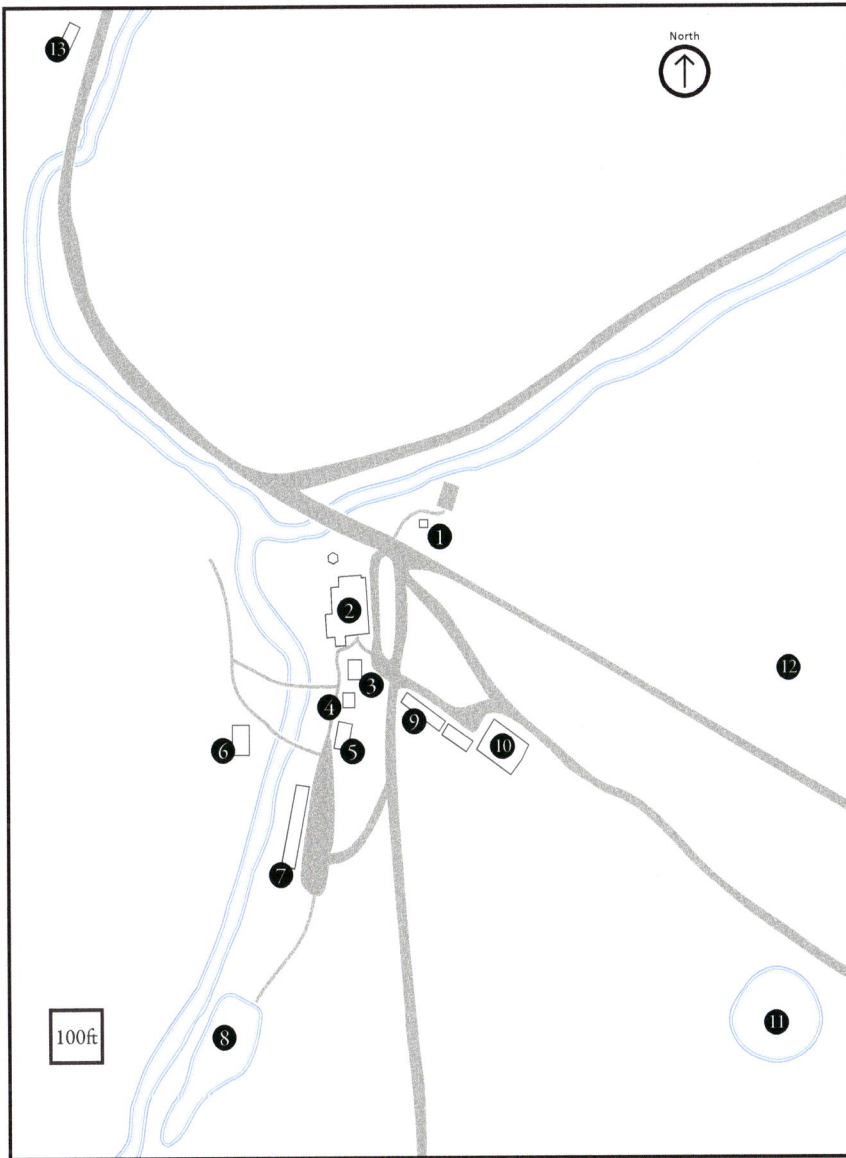

North ↑

100ft

10. The picturesque seven-stall barn, with adjoining corral, was constructed in the earliest years of the White Sulphur Springs Hotel, possibly by Watson Diehl, a master carpenter from the area who specialized in barn-building and is said to have been the master builder of the White Sulphur Springs Hotel. The frequent subject of paintings and publication covers, today the barn serves as the stable for the OCF horse program, which offers trail rides to individuals and groups.

11. Up the road from the barn is the swimming pond created by the Cochrans in 1950. Adjacent to the pond are a barbecue pit, space for outdoor games, a playground area, and a vegetable garden.

12. North of the pond is the site of the planned new OCF Heritage House lodge. Nearby is the "Promise Barn," believed to date back to the 1860s, which will be refurbished for continued use in supporting Heritage House operations.

13. Several hundred feet north of the main White Sulphur Springs building, on the road leading to Highway 96, is the "Fisher House," a structure which was originally the Arlington Cottage Hotel owned by Hezekiah E. May, one of a handful of small inns and boarding houses which were operated in Milligan's Cove prior to the opening of the White Sulphur Springs Hotel. Acquired by OCF from longtime owners Maurice and Joy Fisher, today it is used as a staff residence.

9. The late-1800s bowling alley building, which once also housed the White Sulphur Springs Post Office, a small candy/soft drink counter, and a gas station, continues in use for guests who delight in the old hand-set wooden pins and balls and the two challenging alleys.

R. R. COLVIN.   M. S. COLVIN.

White Sulphur Springs Hotel
Heated Throughout By a Most Modern Hot Water System.

A beautiful retreat among the Pines and Mountains of Bedford County, Penna. A large three-story Hotel with broad Verandas surrounding the same.

The Springs belong exclusively to us. No other hotel or boarding house has the right to the use of this water for its Guests.

The Sulphur and Iron Water combined is unsurpassed. Terms from $7.00 to $10.00 per week. $1.50 per day. Open early and late in the season.

SANITARY PLUMBING.
HOT AND COLD SULPHUR BATHS.

Sulphur Springs, Bedford Co., Pa.,   191

1.

The quiet of evening falls softly,
Over mountain and meadow and hill,
The winds whisper gently together,
While they play o'er the wheat fields at will.

2.

The dainty sweet flower of the wild-rose
Unfolds a pink chalice to view;
And soft in the shadowy grasses
The daisy nods, heavy with dew.

3.

Sweet thro' the hush of the evening
The wood thrush's bugle-note rings
And far in the depths of the forest,
A chorus of bird-voices sings.

4.

The dim dusky aisles of the forests
Are filled with mysterious light.
Very slowly and gently steal onward
The fleet-footed fairies of night.

5.

But softer than ripple of brooklet,
And softer than flutter of wings,
Is the murmuring sound of the pine trees,
That sigh lovingly round White Sulphur Springs.

Bertha S. Grazier
June 28 - 1918.

www.ingramcontent.com/pod-product-compliance
Lightning Source LLC
Chambersburg PA
CBHW061054090426
42742CB00002B/33